# PUSSIFICATION OF AMERICA

*All the best!*
*Nic*

A Book of Interviews, Facts, and Policy Recommendations That If Understood and Implemented, Can and Would Save America!

COPYRIGHT 2012: The Executive and Nic Vila

This book was completely written by the end of September, 2012 and changed not before, or after, Election Day, 2012.


Available at Amazon.com


Kindle version also available from Amazon.com.


Join the conversation @HotPinkBook and www.facebook.com/HotPinkBook

# TABLE OF CONENTS

Preface………….................................................4

Into…………….…………………………..…..8

Chapter 1 – How Our National Manhood Eroded, The Executive's View…………………10

Chapter 2 – How Our National Manhood Eroded, The Executive's Wife's View…………...45

Chapter 3 – The Bastardization of America………………………………………….70

Chapter 4 – How The Pill Screwed This Country………………………………………….87

Chapter 5 – The Cosmo Girl, Now!...................122

Chapter 6 – Men Who Won't Protect and Provide for Their Wives and Families……….128

Chapter 7 – STATE FUNDED POVERTY IS GOING TO KILL US!......................................138

Chapter 8 – Middle Eastern Oil is Bleeding Us Dry! (How We Lost the Inititial Battle for Oil, Then the War)...………………………………144

Chapter 9 – What Must Be Done to Save America……………………………………..148

Chapter 10 – What if..………………………162

## PREFACE

When you are a writer, many take it upon themselves to tell you what your next, fiction story should be; or, they volunteer to tell you about something that really happened and that you "ought" to write about it.

One day, I bumped into this 65 year-old, International Oil Industry Executive (The Executive, or Executive). I have to admit that I really liked the guy because he was a real man's man. The type the world needs: A classic, Robert Mitchum man.

I have to admit, I've always been intrigued with global business and the men and women who possess the skill sets and strength to thrive in global, business action because, well, not everybody can do it. It can, and usually does, grind you like a carrot in a food processor!

In talking with The Executive, I knew I was looking at a John Wayne of the Global Energy Industry.

He asked me about my recent book. I told him. Sure enough, he said, "I got a book for you."

I thought, "Darn, here we go. Another damn memoir about…"

He said, "It's to be called, The Pussification of America, and it is about how this country, and its men, have become pussified, and how it happened."

I said, "Really, how do you mean?" Like everyone else, I already, intuitively knew what he was saying and that he was right; but, being early in the conversation, I wanted to hear about his angle; about what exactly he meant; and, exactly how he thought it happened, and over what time period?

Parenthetically, I had read scholarly and non-scholarly pieces about the slipping of various measures of the fortitude of our country; and, I could easily see our country's loss of status, and that our strategic commitment to classic, traditional values of strength and peace at the same time, had somehow, somewhere, been lost along the way.

And, on a micro level, being a grown man who had a above average understanding of the nature of men and women taught us, directly and indirectly, in the Bible, I had thought much about men and women, and how, in our respective ways, we are both screwed up to such an extent and so ubiquitously, that I had come to realize that I knew only a very, very few man/woman relationships that were, well, of any great good.

So, the executive and I had a seat and I said, "Tell me your view of the whole thing."

He surprised me. He had a view, an explanation, which no one, so far as I had read or heard in media, had said, at least in toto.

We departed. To be honest, I still didn't want to be involved. I had other things to do. But, his explanation of how it happened stuck in my mind and kept nagging me.

After a couple weeks, I called him and said I thought he had something and that I thought it would be worth it to both of us to get together and talk it out. I went to visit. We talked, on and off, for three days.

On the morning of the third day, how to write it hit me and I realized it was something, in fact, that had to be told.

I told him how I thought it should be written, and we agreed.

I thought it would be pretty straight forward, and it is, really. However, for example, his wife hit me with something I didn't see coming. As a woman who had come of age at the beginning of the push of Women's Lib and The Sexual Revolution, it was she who, in only two words, explained to me what has really ruined our country. The two words: The Pill.

Yes, his book title is edgy, maybe even a little crass. But, what is written inside is important, maybe even for the National Security of The United States of America! I'm serious!

I sincerely believe that after you read this little, pink book, you will think we've earned the right to ask you to tell all your friends about it and encourage them to goto our outlets and order, his or her, own copy because for the sake of our country, men and women must read our little, pink book, dialogue about it, and pressure our government officials to take actions prescribed at the end.

After you read our book, I'd bet you'll say to a friend, "Wow, have you read that little, pink book about what's wrong with our country?"

And, I'd bet he or she will ask you, "Which book?"

Then, I'd bet the farm you'll lean in, closely, and whisper, "The Pussification of America!"

Nic Vila

# Introduction

We have purposely chosen to do two things the presentation of our material on the pages of this book.

First, while the standard practice has been to write out a number, e.g., forty-five billion, we've chosen to write out the numerals because Americans need to 'see' the zero's because the numbers associated with our debt and financial problems are getting truly, ridiculously, terrifying!

Second, there are no footnotes or endnotes. We cite, or write the source, right in the copy. No apologies. By now, everyone knows how to Google; to "research;" and/or, verify. And, since our book is being downloaded by thousands (so far), we decided to put the links in the copy.

What has been written here in this little, famous, hot pink book is the truth!

All Americans know it and are growing sick of all this pussified mess the government people have created.

Government people should no longer assume the American people will continue to live with and acquiesce to their malfeasances.

The people, from whom the governments derive powers, are fed up and starting to say, "Hell no! No more!"

# CHAPTER 1

## How Our National Manhood Eroded

### The Executive's View

"You got to remember that in 1945, we had 13,000,000 fighters who had fought and won major victories over Japan, Germany and Italy. They had *stopped* Japanese expansionism, German Nazism and Italian fascism.

The ending of those wars was by unconditional surrender. We won the war: there was no doubting in Germany's mind they had had their asses whipped. There was no doubt in the Japanese mind that they had had their asses whipped; there was no doubt in the Italian fascists' minds they had their asses whipped.

When you fight a war, you fight to win. That's what war is about. If you are not going to fight to win, why fight? The United States had never lost a war since its inception and they had always fought to win!

Someone jumps on you, you fight to beat them; if you're going to jump on somebody, you fight to beat the hell out of them. You fight until they surrender or you have killed them all.

We had millions of men overseas; plus, the whole country of men and women who didn't go off to fight had contributed to victory. However, one byproduct of that war-- because the men were gone off to fight --was that the women started working. So, for the first time, the women felt, 'Well, I can do a man's work.'

When the men came back home, most women went back home to take care of their families. Most became domestic, again. We had the baby boom because women like to have sex with winners and winners like to have sex with women.

The point that must be said, again, is that everybody in the culture, at that time, felt like a winner. But, right after the successful victory of World War II, we got into the Korean conflict: 1950, 1951, and 1952.

McArthur was over there winning in Korea. The Chinese came into it and McArthur advised the president, 'Give me the wherewithal and we'll kick their asses, too!' McArthur was clear. He said, 'If we don't do it now, we'll have to do it later. There is no substitute for victory!'

The Communists had just taken over China in 1949. They were a very weak country at that point.

But they did not want a pro-democracy government on their border because they figured they would have to worry about their people escaping and going for the democratic country--

they wanted North Korean communists on their border.

Therefore, when we got to the Yalu River, the UN forces, which were 80% Americans, 50% of whom were WWII veterans who were used to winning, were told to stop. Can you imagine what went through those WWII American troops minds? 'Stop? Are you kidding us?'

Then, the Chinese communist sent 1 million troops and drove us back to a stalemate line. That's when McArthur told the president, 'You got to give me more men and materials.'

That's when Truman pussied out; he wouldn't let our planes chase the Communist planes back to and across the Yalu river. He wouldn't let us bomb across the river. We started fighting the war to get out of it.

For the first time, the United States of America effectively lost our way. We haven't won a war since.

McArthur told the president, 'There is no substitute for victory!' He had men fighting for him who were used to being victorious but our political leaders let us down.

That non-win, that stalemate, affected our national psyche!

With Korea, you had a group of men and women in the United States who had fought and won against Nazi-ism (which, we thought, was a right war to fight). And, they had fought the Japanese and their atrocities, and fascism.

We were a country of men and women used to righting wrongs.

We were righting a wrong when North Korea jumped on South Korea. South Korea was a democracy; North Korea was a dictatorship. Americans, historically, have believed in what we believe in and we do something; or, we don't believe and do nothing.

If you're right and you go in to fight, you go in like Patton; you go in to kill the sons-of-bitches. That's the only way to fight a war. You go in to win!

Korea was the first time in our history of having to go to war where you could ask, 'Why did we even go in?' We could have just let them have it. Why did we sacrifice all that blood and treasure to end up back where we started?

Korea emboldened the Communist. They saw we were not in it to fight to the end and win. Russia and China's been hard to co-exist with, ever since.

We got out; Truman fired McArthur and appointed a yes man who followed the political line: The U.S. Army is supposed to be nonpolitical. Truman, the man who dropped two atomic bombs on Japan, pussied out!

Then, we elected Eisenhower. He was the General who had beaten Nazi Germany: He had been The Supreme Allied Commander.

Well, first we had the Suez crisis. That's where Egypt took over the Suez Canal, which belonged to the French and the British because they built it. The Israelis, British and French had to take it back from Egypt and Eisenhower refused to back them.

So, Eisenhower's waffling is where you got your Pan-Arabism started, where we didn't back our allies- Number One; and, Number Two, we let Egypt screw over Britain and France and steal their canal they built in Egypt, which Egypt had nationalized for themselves.

We simply didn't back our strongest allies, Britain and France. Then, we told them to get out of Egypt!

Then, continuing the decline in resolve and victory, we had a big uprising in Hungary (many don't remember). The Hungarians asked us to help. They wanted to throw off the Soviet dictatorship that was ruling their country-- thousands of these people were being shot down in the streets. Ike pussied out!

Hell, we had just been involved in Europe. We'd sent hordes of men over there to defeat Nazi Germany. And now, all the sudden, our leader can't get involved in Europe? Baloney!

Hungary, too, affected our national psyche in a negative way.

Back home at that time in the good ole US of A, only one in 50 children were born out of wedlock. These days, it's one-half, if not more.

But, back then, we still had family units. You still had women who respected men. The men had gone off to war and won.

But, all of a sudden, with Korea and the Suez and Hungary, we were no longer winners-- we began to squander our moral high ground.

We began to slip on taking care of our interests. You know, we had thought Nazi-ism was bad but all of a sudden, we started to accommodate communism. All of a sudden, we weren't gonna stand in the yoke of helping people get out of communism. Consequently, millions died in the Soviet Gulags.

When we did take somewhat of a stand as in Korea, we did not follow through. In Hungary, it was the same thing. And, in Egypt, we let the Arabs take over our Western assets. Egypt should've gotten a fair deal out of it. But they had not put up all the monies. The British and the French had.

Later on, you would be able to see the same thing with Carter giving back damn Panama Canal. That's just another example of how we had lost it.

But, back to Eisenhower: What did he decide to do? He was getting a lot of bad press about being a damn wimp, so he decides to send military advisers to South Vietnam, which was 'another' north-south situation just like South Korea/North Korea. Apparently, as a veteran, he thought, 'I can't stand to lose another country. I'll just prop this situation up by sending in military advisors.'

Then, along comes John Kennedy.

Kennedy got us into the Vietnam War. Another war where we were fighting with one hand tied behind our back. The soldiers at that time were the sons of the men who had won the war in Europe and Japan. They were the sons who had listened to their fathers' tales of how America was doing a good thing by righting wrongs by defeating Naziism, Japanese expansionism, and fascism.

These fighters' fathers were encouraging their sons that they should go fight in South Vietnam to keep the Communist from taken over a South Vietnamese democracy. However, our leaders didn't go into that son-of-a-bitch to win, either. They pussied out!

The French had already told us not to go in there if we were not going in to win. Once again, the rules of engagement were against us. We couldn't chase the Migs back into Communist China. So they'd slide in, shoot at us, and run like hell.

North Vietnam's Haiphong Harbor was where 80% of their war materials were coming in and we could have bombed the H20 of it, but we didn't. Leaders were afraid we might hit a Soviet ship.

Years later, the Soviets shot down an unarmed airliner, KAL007, killing hundreds! Evidently, they didn't get the memo.

North Vietnam did not make enough ammunition to fight the damn war. Russia and China were sending all that material to them, bringing it right into Haiphong. We knew it.

All we had to do was close the damn harbor. Our leaders didn't have the balls to do it. We were afraid we might hit a Russian ship: To hell with a Russian ship! We needed a real man running the war! Our kids were getting killed. Somebody needed to end it.

Kennedy wasn't the man to do it. And, he's also the one – while all this Vietnam baloney was going on –who got us into the Bay of Pigs situation, in Cuba.

Once again, we sent a boatload of Cuban exiles down there, three or 4000 of them. We helped them land on the beach and the world knew we were the ones doing it because the Cubans couldn't do it without our help.

We landed them on the beach and here comes the Cuban Migs (piloted by Russians)! Kennedy pussied out-- he wouldn't give 'em any air cover: Poor bastards got shot to pieces on the beach.

Those damn Communists killed thousands of them because we had done everything in half-assed fashion.

Well, everybody says…"The Cuban Missile Crisis…"

There wouldn't have been a damn Cuban Missile Crisis if we would have just taken over Cuba. We had the exiles wanting to do it if we had just supported them. Now, only 90 miles away, we've had this pain in our national butt since 1959.

About this time, American women started to look differently at American men. For thousands of years, man had been the defender of the hearth and home. Women had the men to keep the wolves out of the cave, out of the front door, while she cooked the food and nursed the babies.

That's how families and strong societies start and continue. It's damn true! It's in your genes. It's in our DNA. It's been that way for thousands of years.

Again, we had the Cuban missile crisis, which happened because we didn't back our own people when they tried to invade Cuba. So, Russia thought, rightfully so, that they could do any damn thing they wanted.

It cost the Russians almost nothing to send a few missiles and jets down there. Nothing to speak of compared to the geopolitical and other returns they've enjoyed over the years, since.

The Russians fully expected us to kick them out of Cuba at the Bay of Pigs and take it over. When we didn't, they sent missiles in '62 just to see what we would do, creating the Cuban Missile Crisis.

And, *Oh, Kennedy's strong*, we thought, *He'll show 'em.*

Well, hell naw, he didn't show anybody, anything! He had us over in Vietnam fighting that war so as NOT to win it. He sent mercenaries into Cuba, didn't give 'em full support of The United States, and got them butchered; then, he got himself, and us, into the problem of the Cuban

Missile Crisis because Russia didn't have any fear of or respect for us. They still don't. They know we are a richer economy but they don't respect us as fighters or defenders of the hearth. Putin will just as soon kick America's teeth out!

So, we slid as if downhill on ice, from winning the world's biggest war, to a stalemate in Korea-- not fighting it to win and running off the man that could have won, into South Vietnam. Sadly, everybody knows we lost that son-of-a-bitch.

I mean, the Communists said, 'Okay, we'll let you get out of here. We know your tail is dragging out your damn tracks but we'll let you get out of here. We'll have a truce so you can get your shit out because the South Vietnamese are unwilling to fight for themselves: They're completely pussified now, just like you are.'

The South Vietnamese saw America and all its money and they started pimping dope and whores to our troops, and not fighting for themselves.

The loss was not our troops' fault. Our pussified leaders caused the troops to get disillusioned. It was true in a more subtle way in Korea but everybody understood, 'There are 1 million Chinese troops. How many boys are we willing to lose, so on and so forth.'

But, in Vietnam, no one ever thought we went in to win. I was in my early teens when it all started but I did not want to go. No one I knew did because you could tell the leaders were pussified on the situation. My contemporaries were of the opinion, 'Why do I want to go over there and get my ass shot off for a war that I know we're not in it to win?'

If you want to win a war, one thing you can do when the opportunity avails itself, is close off their supply line. You starve 'em for supplies and win the thing. Our leaders could have done that, if they had wanted.

Our leaders didn't do anything to win Vietnam. So, our troops became very disillusioned. We were doing the fighting for the South Vietnamese. Basically, if they didn't want to free their own country, why the hell were we there? I defy anyone to answer this question to a degree that finally justifies all the deaths of our boys!

Step up and answer!

You know, in other wars for other countries where we helped, the indigenous people fought for their homes and hearths.

For example, we didn't have to worry about the French partisans-- they fought like hell. The Yugoslavian partisans-- they'd claw your eyes out: They wanted it. The Philippine people, the partisans, they fought the Japanese, tooth and nail. Hell, all they wanted was guns and ammo. Keep your damn butter!

In 1956, the Hungarians would have fought if we had armed them. Likewise, in 1968, the Czechs would have fought if we had given them guns instead of letting Russia crush them.

The Afghans ran the Russians out without US Troops. All we did was supply arms. That's a fact, Jack!

Parenthetically, since WWII, our government leaders have been prone to be selectively outraged. For example, they were aghast to learn of Germany's atrocities in 1945; yet, they stood aside while Stalin killed 36 million of his countrymen in his Gulags!

But, back to partisans we *did* help: Their people were on the front line, fighting, violently because war is violent, and best fought when there is a cause in which one believes with all his or her heart. They were on the front lines for their country, their homes and hearths. All these peoples of the world we helped during our eras, well, they all wanted their countries back.

Korea fought but we didn't support them. Then, when the going got tough, we got the hell out.

Again, beginning with World War II, we went from conquering heroes and our women proud of us, to vacillators, not wanting to win anything. Compare us to Israel. They win their wars. They fight to win and shut it down. Then, they get back to work!

We think we are so secure because we're so far away. Well, we're not secure. Al Qaeda showed us that. We are not secure; we're just a long ways away. But, the world is getting smaller, every day.

For example, take Iran. If Iran had a bomb and a missile that could deliver it, well, you better get damn scared because they've got balls. They'd launch the son-of-a-bitch.

They may be lunatics in your mind but in their mind, they are right. They think God is on their side, just like we used to think God is on our side.

We no longer think God is on our side. We don't believe in God like we used to. Our politicians do not believe in God.

We can't even win the war on poverty! We can't win the war on drugs! We haven't won a war since World War II.

Well, I forgot. Wait a minute. We did kick 20 Cubans' assess in Granada. We dog-gone got them! If they had set up a perimeter, history being our guide, we might have divided the island and gave 'em half of it.

But, we didn't get a chance for that move because they fought, but we got 'em. We killed all 20 of them. Of course, they were bulldozer drivers. But no mater, we got the sons'a'bitches. War is hell!

The problem with the damage of our national psyche is if you don't have any self-esteem, it disrupts your fighting forces. Everybody might say, 'Well, the morale of the US military was terrible toward the end of the Vietnam War in the 70s.'

Well, guess what, it sure was and it was the fault of our pussified leaders. The rules of engagement they agreed to got our asses kicked by the Vietcong, who were running around in little straw hats. Heck, we had helicopters; missiles; every kind of napalm; yet, we got our asses handed to us by those little bastards.

And, it was not our troops' fault. It was the fault of our pussified leaders.

The Vietcong were digging tunnels and moving around like rats. They wanted to win it for their country. Our leaders didn't give a damn. They used our troops as mercenaries, without big pay or the booty of war.

We went over there to keep big business and big corporations humming at home. But, the psyche of the 'man in the man' of this country was changing. This country was turning into a different country. Obviously, we had begun to believe were no longer right. Else, we would have gone into these war situations and won them.

If you're right, you're right.

As the psyche of the man was changing, in comes The Pill, giving women the ability to have sex <u>like promiscuous men</u>. With it, came free love and all that. Now, we have the bastardization of America.

----

So, we went to Kuwait. George Bush senior, being wise about world affairs, knew that if we got rid of Saddam, Iran was gonna take it over because they are majority Shiite. So, he didn't.

We did not leave Hitler, Mussolini, or Tojo in power: Why Saddam?

He should have taken Saddam down, kept Iran out; and, gone ahead and taken Iran's nuclear power out, right then and there!

Therefore, that was another stalemate. That was not a US victory. That was a stalemate because we left the man in power. You never leave such a man, in such a situation, in power!

Then, in comes George Bush Junior. He goes over and kicks everybody's ass. But, that's the end of his thinking. He had no game plan. Then, everybody's whining, 'We want a democracy for Iraq.'

Well, we got it. The Shiite are majority. That's what democracy means. The majority rules. It's fundamental.

Then, they said 'We don't want them to rule.' Well, goddammit, they're a majority. We don't want them ruling, yet we want a democracy. Conflicting goals! We lost that war! It ended just like Vietnam.

We got all our people out. Now, it's just a matter of time before Iran takes them over. Or, Iraq comes in under Iran's wing.

We could have preempted the world's current, Iranian conundrum.

And, you might think I'm crazy but we're going to lose Afghanistan. Here's a theory: The only way to win is to kill every son-of-a-bitch in there and repopulate it with illegal aliens from New Mexico, Arizona, Texas, and California. Hell, just give them the country.

Not a bad theory if you really think about it!

It's like this, if you're a Mexican and come across the river and we catch you, we are not going to deport you back to Mexico. Noooooo. We're going to deport your ass to Afghanistan and you are going to work there and have babies or whatever you want to do because there will be no damn, American Welfare Program, or Medicaid over there. There will be no American Social Security.

You'll work, or starve to death. You want a new opportunity? Well, here it is. Poppy fields need planting and tending. And, for money, you folks can sell that shit to Mexico and the Mexican cartels can see if they can get it into the US. Heck, we'll just set up a big ole circle and keep it rolling along.

Speaking of drugs, we could win the war on drugs in 60 days. Here are some theories for you: Only thing it would take would be to deploy the 101$^{st}$ Airborne, with drones, to the border with orders to shoot to kill (and get CNN, et al, to broadcast).

The next step would be to execute anyone with more than the legal minimum of drugs and chop the right hand off anybody caught with drugs (and get CNN, et al, in on that, too).

By the way, having the minimum of illegal substances is like being a little pregnant. 'truth is, you've been having sex with somebody.

Regarding addicts, well, they'd be surprised how fast they would be able to 'un-addict' themselves. And, if they didn't, well, Bucky, we don't need you anyway.

We don't want to support you if you kill all your brain cells and you're in some government run institution costing us $50,000 a year for the next 50 years cause you messed yourself up? Hell no-- live on the street.

Or, here's a theory for you: We'll just put you out of your misery. We can't carry all of these bills for bad morals, anymore.

Once again, it's just like the water buffalo herd: The predators aren't up at the front chasing the healthy, strong buffalo. Hell naw, they're at the back, taking down the weaklings (drug addicts).

They know the sons-of-bitches at the front are mean and strong, that they have pride. An African Water Buffalo can kill a lion in a minute.

That's why lions approach from the back of the heard. He or she chases the old buffalo, or the weak. But, we don't do that anymore in America. The weak ones-- the illiterate and the drains to society, are wrapped in a safety cocoon and we take care of them.

Well, that's fine for the old and/or feeble. But, for the people who can but won't work, all they're gonna do is breed more people that won't work-- that's proven.

We can't win the war on poverty because they are out breeding the money supply necessary for victory!!

That's what happens in any country with exploding social programs-- mark it. That's what happened to Britain, Greece, Spain, and Italy. They cannot tax enough to keep pace. If we keep going like we're going, the same thing is coming to a town or city near you!

The problem with our following that pattern is that there would be no backstop to America going broke!

You get to the stage where we are now, where there's not enough payers to do the paying!

This is the final stages of decline of America because we have lost our maleness. Plain and simple: We have lost our men. They have all been pussified.

The Great Society of the 1960s started this mess.

Lyndon Johnson and his Great Society, when it came out, promised we were going to bring everybody up by the government's bootstraps.

You can't afford to bring everybody up. Our Constitution says that all men are created equal. That does not mean everybody gets the same money. That means every American has the same chance as all others. A man works out from there.

Nobody realized what LBJ was going to do, that he was going to ruin us. He had a unique opportunity for himself with the assassination of Kennedy.

From there, he acted with the cloak of Kennedy wrapped around him as if to say, 'This is what John would've wanted.'

That's how he got the Voting Rights Act, The Great Society, and all his liberal politics rolling, which was very surprising because he was a Texan from a conservative district (conservative at that time).

But, at the same time, he was pursuing the Vietnam War and he just didn't have the nuts to do it all. He could've won that war. If he had, he would've been considered one of the nation's best presidents.

LBJ could've won Vietnam as easily as lost it. We had 500,000 troops over there. All he had to do was finish it-- bomb Hanoi to the ground. We dropped two nuclear bombs on Japan. Why couldn't we have bombed Haiphong Harbor?

With the social things he accomplished, if he had coupled them with a victory in Vietnam, he would've been celebrated as a Lincoln-type president. But, he pussied out. It all comes back to the point that he was not man enough to do what needed to be done.

Diabolical men and countries should know not to mess with us. We ought to be like Teddy Roosevelt-- we ought to walk around softly and carry a big stick. To the bad men and countries in the world we should say, 'If you mess with us, we're gonna hit you in the head with this big stick, and enough times you can't get back up. We're not gonna tap you, we're gonna kill your asses, probably wipe you off the face of the earth.'

The rest of the world is a little scared of us. We have guns in our closets. We kill more people with guns every year than all the other countries, combined. We like the guns. We like killing people.

That's what DNA is telling real men, right now. That doesn't really go in 50 years. We need to search ourselves, find those genes, and re-activate them.

---

Today, in the US of A, women have ascended and taken the spot men once had because the men no longer have any fight left in them.

Again, during WWII, women learned they could do a man's job. Most women knew that but it was really affirmed in WWII. After the war, some of them stayed in the workforce.

But later, along came the sexual revolution. As we've said, now over 50% of the babies are born out of wedlock: Women don't think they need men.

Men don't have the work ethic they had. Many won't work at all. They won't protect the household; they won't step up to their obligations to take care of their children. Consequently, women ask, 'For what do I need a man?'

If it wasn't for the need for procreation, they wouldn't need a man, at all. And, some women have decided they don't need men for sex, either. They use their sex toys, or get another woman to do the job.

Throughout history until now, one or 2 men out of a 100 turn into pussies Now, you might have four or 5 out of a hundred who still remember they are men.

The rest of them are afraid. You can't tell a Jewish joke anymore; you can't tell a black joke anymore; blacks can't tell white jokes; and, heaven forbid, you can't tell a Muslim joke. We're just about to where we can't function.

You can't smoke; you can't ride a motorcycle down the highway without a helmet; you gotta have a seatbelt on in the car; they'll tell you what size Cola you can drink.

But, you know, people that get on a motorcycle without a helmet and kill themselves, they need to be killed. They're stupid sons'a'bitches. Heck, send them out.

You know, I've got a brain. If I get on a motorcycle, I'm going to put on a helmet.

When I get in my car, there should not be a state law that I have to buckle my safety belt. The ones that don't, probably need to be in heaven, or wherever they're going. We shouldn't be burdened with stupid people.

America has given all her people the chance to go to school. Everybody in this country, especially the blacks for the past 50 years, has had a chance go to school. Schools are begging for students. But if you don't avail yourself of the opportunity, that's not my problem. I should not have to support you for the rest your life because you would not go to school when you had the option. A real man and a real woman avail themselves of the opportunities that come along.

You're not going put me in the male chauvinist pig category. I have a wife who is as independent as she wants to be and we have lived together for 50 years. We make decisions together; we do things together; but, there are things that men are supposed to do, and things that women are supposed to do. It's in the Bible. The Bible explains it.

A good wife is more precious than rubies and pearls. A good woman, you should treat better than yourself. When you marry that woman, you forsake all others, including your parents. Your wife is your other half. A husband is to love and protect! A wife, honor and obey! Do we even remember classical, Biblical vows?

I'm not advocating a woman be barefooted and pregnant and in the house all the time. More of them need to be 'un-pregnant', frankly.

But, I do say women need to remember the man's role in society and give it back to them. Funny thing, I guess they're going to have to give it back because men don't seem capable of taking it back.

But we will –the pendulum always swings, back and forth. Right now, a woman in Saudi Arabia understands she can't drive. She must wear a veil and be subordinate, seriously subordinate, to her husband (or father).

Over there, in Saudi-- I've been there many times --that's where the pendulum is still swung way back to the man side.

But, in the Western world, there's a medium place the pendulum can rest. That's what made this country great.

Women came to the frontier like men did. Women worked right 'long side their husbands and the husbands had a respect for her that did not, could not, exist for women in many, other parts of the world because the conditions of Western thought and common law-based, Republic form of government and economic opportunity, did not, and cannot exist, in almost all other countries of the world.

Married men and women in historic America are, or can be, domestic and economic partners in ways not available in any, other place on the earth. Women in America have always, historically, worked right along-side their husbands in a very, unique relationship. Marriage and family can be a real partnership in America!

But, now women are taking the man's role by default because the men are not accepting the responsibility. I think it all started with our defeatist political agenda in this country, decades ago.

You can track it: The Korean War; the Vietnam War. Heck, the Cold War was another stalemate. We just outspent them. Any pussy can spend money! Especially when others—taxpayers – are creating the money through their labor!

Further, we're losing in Afghanistan and Iraq; domestically, were losing the war on poverty; the war on drugs. We've spent trillions of dollars getting beat-- why?

Speaking of the war on poverty, we should say, 'Ok, we're going to give you a check and you're going to go to school. Plus, you're gonna take the piss test. If you're on drugs, you're not going to school because evidently, you have enough money to buy drugs. So, you should have enough money to make it.'

'If you get two or three illegitimate babies, you are going to pay for them. Or, we gonna put your ass in jail; and, you're gonna get a jail job to pay for them.'

That's not cruel and unusual punishment. That's stepping up to the plate. If you don't want to do it, *man*, society is gonna step up and make you do it: Cowboy up, *man*.

See, used to, 100 years ago, if you were a dead beat, the community would visit and tell you, 'You need to take care of your family.'

You can't criticize that. I don't care if he said he had depression or something like that. He was a pussy, that's what it boiled down to.

Used to, the government didn't have to get involved in taking care of people's families. The community got involved in making sure you took care of your family. I mean, there were probably limits on that, but not large limits.

In the 60s, that's when you begin to see the boys with her hair hanging down to the asses, smoking dope and burning their draft cards. You would not have burned your draft card in World War II.

Your friends and neighbors would have shamed you. Men were embarrassed if they weren't in the Armed Services. There had to be something wrong with them. Or, they were less than manly.

When I grew up, ranchers and farmers were excluded from the draft because the country had to have someone raising the beef. There were people in factories, mainly engineers and such, they wouldn't draft them because they were in critical industry. In the Vietnam War, the only ones that seemed to get drafted were the ones who couldn't buy congressmen or something like that. It was a complete reversal from prior wars.

For the first time, a lot of guys didn't want to go because they knew we were not going over there to win it. You think these guys wanted to go and be killed for some South Vietnamese who wouldn't fight for himself? No!

Everybody knew our political leadership were not over there to win. Everybody knew that. We knew that from the get go. It's not something put on the bulletin board. We just knew it.

I was draft age at the time. I didn't want to go-- I would've gone if I had been drafted -- but I didn't get drafted and I was not going to volunteer.

If I would have been drafted (and shipped over there), I'da been just like anybody else: I'da tried to keep myself safe for my year, then get out and back home.

That's when men really started to turn. That's when you started having these large numbers of gays and lesbians.

The women have given up on men; the men are tired of competing. That's the plain and simple truth! Many now say, 'I'd rather perform felatio on a man, or have a man perform it on me, that to have a woman perform it on me. I can't compete with these women. I can't support one. I don't have the wherewithal.' With rare exception, that's where we are.

And remember, Jane Fonda went over to North Vietnam, sat on the barrel of an antiaircraft gun aimed to shoot down American pilots and said, basically, 'I don't see why we're fighting these wonderful people.' I lived through that. She came home, and there was no punishment meted out to her.

Actually she was given a better career. She was an antiwar activist. Did you see that in World War II? Hell no. We didn't even have that in the Korean War. That's where we started our serious, downward slope. We should not have let that woman get by with it. She should've been put in Leavenworth for treason; that's a crime in this country-- supporting an enemy combatant.

There are some states that Fonda never went to for years and years. There are some out there who still can't stand that woman, especially, the ones who had sons and daughters over there. Here was this bitch, the first, famous woman showing us this new womanhood, basically saying, 'I got balls; I'm gonna go over there and aid and abet the enemy of my country.'

We were at war with those people. You know, they hung people for that in WWII. She was in Hanoi, in country, itself, not sitting on a boat-- she was sitting on an antiaircraft gun, aimed at American planes and pilots.

That was the first, new-American woman.

Then, came Carter, another national disgrace who made us all hang our heads. Not that he was a sorry president, he was, but with him in the White House, the enemy took our embassy and held it for a year and a half, along with approximately 400 people. When he finally did something, it was so ill planned, the team barely got to Iran, and never to Tehran.

Meanwhile, while we were messing up like that, Israel, an itty-bitty country with six million population, took a small number of their troops to Entebbe, Uganda, 3,600 miles away from Jerusalem, and got their hostages out. We couldn't fly a hundred and fifty miles from an aircraft carrier and get our people out. Then, Carter just backed down.

My solution for our Carter, hostage situation would have been to send a message to them that said, 'We're landing an American, 747 at Tehran International, tomorrow afternoon. It will be there at four o'clock. On your end, you all better hope nothing happens to it. You better have all emergency crews out there and coddle this operation on your end. You may want to line the side of the runway with pillows and bales of hay, you don't want <u>anything</u> to happen to this airplane, I'm telling you. You have our people there. The men need to be freshly shaved. The women need to have new dresses and hairdos, and all our people better be on that jet by five o'clock, safe and sound.'

'Then, we'll turn that son-of-a-gun around and takeoff. You better put some fighter escorts etc. up, or we'll bring some, and you all better make damn sure nobody messes with the plane-- it better get back to Saudi Arabia. <u>If this goes right, we won't kill about a half a million of you suckers.</u>'

'If that doesn't happen, rain, fire, and damnation are gonna fall on your heads until you say it is Ok to send that plane. Until you say yes, we're gonna show you what Satan really looks like, Ayatollah! We gonna start where you live and level that place. We're gonna glass the joint! We're gonna send cruise missiles right on top of your head, right up your ass.'

'Let our people go! Just like in the Bible: Let our people go! We're not playing with y'all. You shouldn't have messed with our people. Let them go.'

But, they knew they would get away with it. Why? Because we were a nation of pussies. Our political leaders are all pussies. When you get one that halfway speaks his mind, he's vilified in the national press.

NBC, ABC, CBS, CNN, you name it. Anybody that says anything that is halfway macho, well, he is a warmonger. We should fight when we're right, fight and get it over with. They don't say Khomeini and Iran or anybody else is a warmonger. Yet, when our embassies are attacked, we can't say anything about revenge? No way. No more!

'75 was when Vietnam fell and we've been getting more and more liberalized, more pussified, ever since.

Remember, the 1968 Democratic convention when antiwar demonstrators shut it down? That's why Johnson didn't run again. It would have mattered to win the war and the war had run over him. The war whipped his ass.

It's plain and simple: We've gone from being a country that was strong and admired, full of heroes, to a country where we're all muffins and will accept anything.

After World War II, all the men came back and the country boomed. The economy retooled. Cars; washing machines; we had the GI Bill.

The G.I. Bill was one of the best bills this country ever had. It gave every fighting man a chance to go to school. We were breeding like flies because conquering heroes like women and women like heroes!

I'm telling you, if you go whip somebody's ass in a bar, some woman is gonna want to sleep with you. They like men. Thus, the best selling, 50 Shades of Grey.

If I were a woman, I would want to be treated like a woman. We need to clear up all this women's Lib. That was a small percentage of the American women. And, it still is.

Abortion, I'm all for it because anybody can make a legitimate mistake. We don't need unwanted, illegitimate bastards running around. Let's get rid of them.

Here's a theory for you that would curb the costs to our society of all these illegitimate babies: Make it legal that from conception to two years old, a baby can be aborted at any time. So, for example, after a year if it's too much trouble supporting the baby, take it to a clinic and let them put it to sleep. Why stop at birth?

This may come. This liberal society we have, the woman may be able to get rid of them up to two years. Mom can't afford another one, so let's get rid of them up to two years old.

Since I'm Catholic, you'd think I would be against abortion. I'm not.

---

Back to immediate, post-World War II, that's when everybody was feeling good and wanted to give the kids everything. We were doing good as a country. We were the most affluent country in the world. So, all these girls and boys were given everything by their mamas and daddies.

Consequently, when these little boys did marry, they couldn't satisfy their women because they couldn't give them all the things daddy had given them: 'Daddy would buy me a new pair of shoes; I want a new pair of shoes.' The poor boy might say, 'Well, honey, we don't have the money.' So, the girl goes back home to daddy.

They were spoiled beyond belief. It affects us up to this day. That's one reason there are so few, successful marriages, now.

Back when we were in the cave, women wanted to breed with the best hunter. Why? Because the woman rightly thought, 'He can take care of my off spring.'

They didn't breed with pussies. The pussified man didn't get to have sex because if you can't take care of your family, you are useless, and deep down, a woman knows that.

You were abandoned by the tribe. That's a fact. If you couldn't take care of your family, you weren't eligible to be married. That's why in Africa and some, other countries, they have initiation rites (as the American Indians did). If you can't pass them, you're not allowed to get married. There's a reason for that. There are certain physical stamina tests you have to be able to pass to entitle you to marry and breed. If you can't pass them, you are passed over, you don't get a wife. Plain and simple.

That's why in their countries there's a price, a sum of money, to buy your wife. That shows the family that you will be able to support her. If you can't provide the price--whatever the going bride price is --then you're not a good provider. It's in the genetics. It's in your DNA. That's the way it's been for thousands of years.

That's how to weed out the inferior. I'm sorry; that's just the way it is. We've been trying to change that in a matter of a handful of decades.

Look, the Huns did it. They were still men. They were not worried about getting in touch with their inner feelings down at the Coliseum. They weren't lying up, eating grapes at the Senate. No, they came down and said, 'We need to kill some folks and take some women and eat tonight.'

I can just hear the captain of the Huns, 'No one has anything to eat tonight. Come on, we got to go kill some sons'a'bitches and steal their food because we don't grow crops. No, our way of living is to plunder. We have to go kill somebody.'

Rome said, 'Come kill us. We're pussified enough, now!' Rome was pussified because of social welfare. No one wanted to stand watch.

There were men in the Civil War.

Have you ever seen a reenactment of a Civil War battle? You see how close they were? Well, I'll tell you, man, I don't know if I could have done it if they had told me to march towards their line and '…they're gonna be over there about 20 yards and you start shooting at each other till somebody hollers calf rope.' That took some damn balls. I'm dead serious.

They killed thousands every day. You try that today. You see how many men get up on that line.

Women have a primal urge to reproduce with the strongest male. If they can't find one, they just as soon take care of themselves. That's where we are. That's what women are doing these days.

Woman after woman I've talk to—and, I've conducted scores of interviews in researching this book –all say, 'I can't find a man.'

Women and girls tell me, 'You just can't imagine what's out there, today. Men won't work. Very few are real men.'

So, why are all these women having babies when they don't have to? The sexual revolution made it come about. You can talk around it all you want. The Pill liberated women, sexually.

So, why, now, are half our babies born out of wedlock?

Because of woman's primal urge for a baby; and, at the same time, they have the brains to know that they don't want some weak man (except to get pregnant when they want to).

You may not hear about that on Dr. Phil, but that's what's going on.

So, The Pill and The Sexual Revolution gave women the ability to have sex without consequence (they thought). The bastardization of America started coming in after the Vietnam War when we became a nation of losers, domestically, and the men just gave up.

But again, women really want a real man. But, there are not enough real men. That's the problem; why else would so many have a baby out of wedlock unless they can't find a man who's going to be strong and take care of it?

If a woman is going have to take care of herself, well, she'll get the baby and forfeit the man because she'd have to take care of him, too. I'm serious, that's what they tell me. I've had several tell me that. 'Why do I want a man?' they ask.

Look, there are three of them over here in this local business. The husband, or the boyfriend, drives them up in the woman's car so she can go to work. The males go back home and drink beer all day and come back and pick them up; that is, if they don't forget them. That's the kind of men we've got now. That's black and white males, by the way.

The more affluent do the same: Their jobs and cars are just better and newer!

This is the way it is nowadays. Bastardization is a black and a white problem. The numbers are really close.

You can't get rid of the girls' drive to reproduce. It's not going away. Thousands of years are inbred in her to reproduce. Women feel the urge to have a baby and they are going to get someone to give them one. But, they don't have to take the daddy, anymore.

If that's not the case, then explain to me why they're having babies? With birth control, they don't have to have them. Birth control is readily available to everyone for six dollars per month.

Again, Dr. Phil won't be telling you this. Your psychiatrist won't be telling you this-- that's just the way it is.

You can't make what's being said in this book pretty. This book has not been approved by a psychiatrist and it won't be on Oprah's Reading List.

As they say, 'Somebody has to tell the mama she's got an ugly baby!'

As Walter Cronkite said, 'And that's the way it is.'"

# CHAPTER 2

## How Our National Manhood Eroded

### The Executive's Wife's View

*Regarding Helen Gurley Brown's book, <u>Sex and the Single Girl</u>, and her confusing duplicity:*

*"But when she writes this book, she herself has already married David Brown. Do the same rules apply when she, and not some other, easily stereotyped woman, plays the role of the wife at home? It seems not. The married man/single woman trope becomes, in a sense, Helen Gurley Brown's stock in trade, part of what she would carry into her tenure at Cosmopolitan magazine and throughout many, if not most, of her future writings. Yet she and David explain, in a number of interviews and writings, that infidelity has no place in their marriage. 'David is convinced,' his work partner Dick Zanuck stated two decades into the marriage, 'that if Helen caught him having an affair, she'd kill him. I mean really kill him.' As Zanuck suggests, two separate Helens exist, one the perpetual single girl who cares not a whit for that unfortunate character, the wife, and the other the grown-up married woman who is that wife and could no better than anyone else weather the storm of marital infidelity. The issue for Helen Gurley Brown was not so much that her life changed after marriage but rather that she seemed trapped afterward, culturally, by the figure she cultivated so*

*carefully and defended so vigorously in and after* <u>Sex and the Single Girl</u>*."*

<u>Bad Girls Go Everywhere</u>, *by Jennifer Scanlon, page 77.*

----

"We were reared on little farm in Texas.

We raised everything we ate except flour and sugar.

My dad had a garage.

Most everybody had a problem paying their bills.

He had a lot of trade credit and it was a big treat to go to town and buy flour and sugar because in picking which flour sack, I was picking the material for my next dress.

So, we were reared sort of poor. We provided much for ourselves: We churned our own butter from milk from our cows, those type things.

Then, my dad got a job with an oil company and we moved to New Mexico. Economically, we did much better, there.

He went to work as a mechanic for a company owned by Gulf. Later, he went into production in their gasoline plants.

We had a much better life, then. We got a new car and we had plenty of food that we did not have to grow or produce.

Politically, I wasn't really aware in my young years. I remember my parents talking some about the depression, but that's about it.

I remember them saying that during the depression, my father worked in a syrup mill and that he would work for a bucket of sorghum syrup he would trade in the evening for what he needed and could get in exchange. I do remember they had some horror stories to tell.

I remember that my mama always had a fetish for shoes because she grew up without them. When she died, she had a closet as big as a standard room and there were shoes from floor to ceiling, probably over 100 pair.

I remember she'd have an occasional yard sale and would get rid of some. Interestingly, when she died, none of the shoes in her closet had tags on them. She had worn every pair, some more than others, but she had worn each.

After the 50's, she got back into collecting China and silverware she hadn't had for a long time. She had none growing up (because her family had been poor). Like my father's family, too, they had come into America through North Carolina, and then they migrated into Mississippi.

My mother remembers her father chopping up the dining room table and furniture for fires in the winter because it was so cold in the house they lived.

----

I was married when the Women's Lib Movement started. At the time it started in the 60's, our lives were different than what they were pushing. We still lived fairly simply.

Drugs started coming out along about that time, too. But we were secluded from them. We lived on a ranch in oil country. Drugs didn't come into conversation with anybody in our world until the 80's or so.

When you lived where and how we lived, where it was rural and everybody was always working hard to make it, we weren't touched by drugs and the Lib movement for quite some time.

Back then in the 60's, if the woman worked, the family was looked down upon. And, the man was considered to be a poor provider and husband.

But, my husband is kind of liberal in some ways. I think if I had really wanted to work, he would have conceded to it.

----

As I got older and we had children, more of my friends did not marry (and had to work and make their own living).

However, some who were married started to work but I thought, 'Who is keeping your kids?'

Many of the married women who went to work didn't have good parents, themselves, so there were no other family members to look after their kids when they worked. I thought the ones whose husbands could afford to support the family were making a mistake.

Some of them said they wanted to be something more than 'just a housewife' and 'a mother'. The revolution had started to make those classic things to be looked down upon, to be things that made women inferior.

I don't know where that idea came from. I've never looked into who got that ball rolling.

A lot of women worked to help accrue money for family goals. For example, to start a business; get a summer home, etc. Most waited until their kids were old and disciplined enough for the kids to spend some time alone (unsupervised).

There were many big mistakes. I'm not saying women shouldn't work but I'm saying your kids have got to come first. If you don't educate, socialize, and rear your kids right, it creates risks for them and society.

It's a problem, today. I have women who work for me who have one, 2, 3 children and they send them to daycare. They are only with them a few hours per night. I don't think that is enough.

I think the difference in daycare and what I did is what went into my kids' minds. I went through everything. I listened to their music; I went through their books; I knew what they were doing in school. These things are not done today, not like they were done in past generations.

When I was a mother rearing my boys, it was my responsibility and I took it very seriously. I knew what the schools were teaching; I knew what was on TV and what they were trying to watch and listen to. I checked out Van Halen, Journey, and Eric Clapton, all of them!

We were overseas for much of my boys' teenage years. When we returned to the states, all that music and culture was coming on strong. I had gone back to college to finish my degree. It was tough to do and took hours out of my day, but I went through all that music, and so forth: My husband and I listened to it all. Most of my peers did, too. We were concerned about what was being pushed at our children. Parents today are not doing what we did, at least to the same degree and with the same intention.

Today, there's so much on TV; then, there's the phones and the Internet, and the Internet can be accessed in various ways. And, I haven't even mentioned Facebook and the other social media outlets. Oh, my God!

I realize that in some ways, it is more difficult these days with all these modern gadgets, but it must be done. Further, I think the realization of the need to supervise children has been lost in the majority of our society. Children's minds must be protected and directed to the correct, Classical, age-appropriate things.

I've done much work in charity groups. The families in need of help must bring in their household bills and let the charity check things out in order for the needy family to receive help. All the charities with whom I've worked do it that way. All the legit charities do this.

Almost without exception, the families have this enormous cable bill. When I would ask if they could cut the cable bill out, the woman would almost always say, as if from a script, 'Well, what am I going to do with my kids?'

The cable is the babysitter!

This is a fundamentally different way of rearing kids! Evidence all around us screams that it is ruining our children!

Setting aside arguments for and against and the difference in the pressures on families and mothers today, notice the elements of instruction, direction and protection in the routines of rearing when we reared our children:

We had breakfast at the table together in the morning. When they came in from school in the afternoon, they had free time from about 2:30 or 3, until 4:30. Then, they came in, bathed, dressed and we had dinner, together, about seven. After dinner, we'd sit down with their books. My husband and I both helped with homework but I did more than he because he had other responsibilities.

I cooked three squares a day and we sat around the table together to eat. There was no television watching from the table and we actually talked.

They had to be in the bed by 9:00 PM. If they finished their homework early enough and had time to spare before bed, we'd watch a movie, something like a John Wayne or other, classic movie (any solid movie with good values). Sometimes, if all had gone well and the movie ran over, they got to bed at 9:30. That was Ok in the larger scheme of things.

Such was our routine for years when we lived overseas.

----

In their early-mid teenage years, we had to move to Indonesia for business. The practice in our industry was to send your children to boarding school in Singapore. We did that, then realized we had lost all control, all ability to impact and direct our children, and all knowledge of what they were really doing.

My husband and I talked about it and came to the obvious conclusion that for the sake of our children and family, we had to return to the USA. It was a huge decision as my husband had to turn down a promotion that would have included an enormous pay and prestige raise.

The drugs in Singapore were getting to be big time. Our family was not immune. It could've become a problem and ruined one or both of our boys, and our family.

This might put the problem in perspective: In 1975, the American Embassy had to charter a 747 to get 343 American children out of Singapore. They were facing jail time for drug possession.

----

I feel I must tell you that my husband and I spanked our children. I fear many parents no longer understand spanking. Our experience was that you had to much less than you expected because once you get the precedent set, the fear of it is a powerful deterrent.

Sure, the boys would push me like I would try to push my mother when I was growing up. I would spank them and like my mother before me,

I'd bring in my husband if I had to. Boy, if daddy got them, 'O Brother!'

Our results were typical: By the time our boys were eight or nine years old, they were well disciplined and no longer required as much disciplinary attention.

----

As we reared them, we did everything as a family. We played card games together. We taught both boys tennis and we played together all the time.

They played tennis until they were 30 years old. Their wives did not know how to play. We told them, 'Well, you better learn.'

Tennis was a big thing for us. Even when they were adults, we would all come home after work, grab racquets and hit the court. It was a good thing for us. It might not be tennis for everyone but it needs to be something, several things, done together to keep the family knit tightly: It's very important!

The only thing, which is not a bad thing, is that since we were so close, it was a little hard for our daughters-in-law to fit in, at first.

----

We came back to the USA in 1980. I experienced culture shock.

I had to pump my own gasoline! I didn't know how at first and it was embarrassing. The reason was cultural: I had not driven in years because where we had lived it wasn't a good idea for a foreigner to drive a car. You could get in big trouble if something happened.

The boys experienced more culture shock than I did. They couldn't believe how the kids acted.

All their peers went to rock concerts *by themselves*, all the time. I told our boys we were not going to let them do that! And, we didn't. Finally, they really wanted to see Eric Clapton (in concert).

So, my husband and I bought tickets for the whole family, and off we went! Oh, my God. What an experience. The bongs were going around. They probably went around the room 100 times. There was pill popping; bottles of whiskey everywhere; and, cops were everywhere, watching the whole thing. It amazed us. The culture and things that had developed while we were away, simply blew our minds.

I went to the restroom during that concert and there were girls snorting cocaine off the floor. The counters were full of purses, bags and other things, so they snorted off the floor. It blew my mind!

I had never really been around drugs. I was aware there was a problem but I didn't realize the magnitude, or the culture that had developed. Even to this day, I've never had a joint of marijuana, or anything, and I'm not about to start now.

I'm not stupid. I knew my kids tried marijuana in Singapore. But, by contrast, the scene in America blew our minds. We were truly shocked!

In Singapore, we were so tight knit that drugs could not get a hold. A family must get, and stay, tightly knit!

What we saw in America upon our return was that kids were not supervised! Therefore, their families were not tightly woven enough to keep the trouble out.

----

The reason I knew a little of the drug problem in the US was because while in Singapore, I had an American friend whose family came home to the states in the 70's (well before we did). Their son was 15 or 16 and he got so badly into drugs that his father told him he had to go to military academy.

He went to an academy and before long, he got into trouble there, too. The school was about to throw him out and his father told him, 'If you get thrown out school, you're on the streets. You're not moving back home. We're not putting up with it, anymore. We're not living that way.'

She said he had been horrible at home before the academy. She said he threw constant fits. She said they couldn't control him and they never knew where he was.

### Women's Lib

As I watched the bra burning days, I realized women were wanting to come into their own and be equal with men. It's not possible. It's not natural for women to be equal with men. In my opinion, it's not a God-given thing.

Women can be as astute as men mentally and intellectually but they can't match them physically (not including infrequent, isolated, anomalous cases of a physical superwoman).

Put it this way, a woman wouldn't last ten runs as a halfback in the NFL. Or, put a woman at linebacker in the NFL and see how long she lasts before they wheel her out on a stretcher. Good grief!

God had his reasons for this. And, I think God's, gender distinctions are the place of the balance in marriage. You have to have respect for the differences in sexes.

I did not have a problem with the man being the man and the woman being the woman. I think that's how it ought to be. There is something devastating to both men and women about emasculating a man.

Economically, I realize many women make more money than their husbands and that their husbands might stay home and keep the kids in that situation. Sometimes, a woman can make more money in her industry than a man can in his.

However, there is a principle that operates in life that cannot be denied: Men are fulfilled when they provide for their wives and families. It's primordial.

Back when I grew up and married, it was a different world than we have today. Men wanted (and were supposed) to provide for their families and if they didn't, they were considered scum. People looked down upon them and they were talked about.

Even in my own family, my dad had a couple of sisters who married men who couldn't keep a job. We were always taking food over and helping in other, various ways. Everybody thought it was horrible. This guy had six or seven kids. He couldn't take care of his wife, or them.

All my girlfriends wanted a strong man to be in the lead in the way men were designed to lead. They wanted marriage; they wanted home life.

The Women's Liberation Movement went too far. I told my girlfriends it would.

The drug revolution was already underway and I think it (and porn) merged and it all took off (I think a big driver of the drug thing was those poor guys coming back from Vietnam all screwed up: Woodstock, and so forth)!

Women's Lib was being pushed. All the magazines pushed it.

Cosmopolitan really pushed it, especially the sex side of it.

Cosmo is still at it, today. I haven't read one in years but I picked one up the other day and it said something about 'If your grandmother or your mother'...and I thought, *They're selling the same thing*! Truly, as the Bible says, there is nothing new under the sun!

The pill did a lot of things, good and bad. On the good side, a married woman could relax and more fully enjoy sex with her husband.

On the bad side, women could be as sexually active as promiscuous men because back then, before the pill, condoms were not reliable. They tended to bust.

It should have been expected that the The Pill opened up a new world of promiscuity for single women. Cosmo and other print media were pushing a raucous lifestyle of unabated sex and affairs with married men. Cosmo was the leader in telling women everything they needed to know about how to do all things (sexual).

I've only had sex with my husband. I probably won't ever have sex with anybody else. I never went for the promiscuity. Believe me, I could have but never did.

It was always inconceivable to me to have sex with someone who you don't know how many people they'd slept with. I just couldn't. Classically, it's morally wrong. It's also disrespectful to your partner/spouse. If you must have sex with someone else, then you should set your partner down and say, 'Look I'm gonna go have sex with somebody, I'm leaving.'

To have a clandestine affair is low down, and dirty.

And living together, everybody does it now. I guess doing so, economically speaking, is good for some people. There's no commitment. That's what worries me about that.

You know they're gonna live together and have sex and maybe have a baby. And they do have children together but they're not married.

This one girl, she has a three-year-old daughter whose father has now turned into a huge drug addict. Well, the baby is listed in her name because the baby came out of wedlock.

We are starting to have a country of bastards.

Classically, a bastard is a child without the father's name. Bastards are everywhere.

I know that sometimes, a woman will make more money than a man, her husband, if, for example she goes into a profession that pays more than his industry pays him for what he does. I do not know what to do about that; however, somewhere along the way, men missed the boat-- I don't know what happened but they missed the boat.

I don't know where they missed the boat. It's as though they're not driven to work. Their work ethic of old has been lost.

Now, you can go to the big city and you see them pick up briefcases and haul ass off to the office: I'm not sure what they're going to do, but they're off to do something.

However, you go to rural areas and you see these guys who just don't want to get up and go. I don't know what happened. I was raised in a very rural area and if you didn't work, you didn't eat.

I understand that some of the rural areas have lost their manufacturing facilities and other businesses; maybe they went overseas or out of business. I can see every morning, cars busting up the roads, heading over to the big city, and I know that many of those are going because there are fewer jobs in the smaller places. That's a problem I don't know what to do about.

Our government, Democrat and Republican alike, have farmed everything out to other places around the world and done all sorts of trade deals-- they've cut our throats, I know. But again, the work ethic of the men is not as strong as it was when I grew up.

When I grew up, during hard times, when whatever you did for a living was negatively impacted, you got out there and did whatever you had to do. You'd open a café; a gas station; you figured out what you could work in and you did it, somehow.

You got out and got a job at some plant. Something. You got out, and did what you had to do. Now, you might argue it's worse than other times. But, that does not wipe out the fact that the work ethic is not as good among men as it was when I grew up.

When I was young, it was every girls dream to go to college. When I got married, my husband's college came first. The major breadwinner went first. I went later.

I went back to school at the end of the 70's, or early 80's. The push for higher education was always there in our age group because you have to be smart; you just can't sit there and let your mind go to hell in a hand basket.

My husband says that the men went to fight World War II, Rosie the riveter went to work and when the man came home, she went back home and into domestic life. To that I say, 'Kinda sort of, she did.'

My husband's mother was a classic example of what I'm saying. That whole family went over during the war-- husband, brothers, everybody. She worked while they were gone but when her husband came home, she continued. Everybody said, 'Oh, lady.'

My mama continued to work, too. My mama was a hell of a smart lady. She took over the post mistress job there in that little town. She loved it. My dad had a problem with it. She told him, 'Now, this is the way it's gonna be. I don't have kids at home. I'm gonna get out of here.'

But, she was smart. My father was probably educated through the eighth grade. But, mother had some college, I don't know how much; but gosh, she was a financial wizard. She had a knack for numbers.

I have a degree in psychology and a degree in interior design. I earned the psych degree first. When I got into clinical, I said to hell with it, I'm not doing this every day. It bothered me. I would have to work with some criminal nut-job and I would think, *I don't care why you molested your little three-year-old. You just put your nuts up here on the table and I'll cut 'em off.'*

So, I got a 'fru fru degree,' LOL, as they say: I earned an interior design degree!

I think a lot of what is wrong with this country today is the sexual revolution. I really think it is at the core of a lot of this ruination, this pussification of America.

I know a lot of women, smart ladies, that were sexually active and had kids, one by one father, one by another– I'm not talking about black women. I'm talking about white women. One of the women I'm thinking of, well, one father doesn't pay his child support, the other does but she has to work to make it up the difference. Now, she is married and seems to be in a good relationship, but all that sexual activity came back to talk to her, as they say. She had been screwing everything that walked, just like the promiscuous men she was doing it with. She became as they were.

And of course, when it comes time to marry, like a young man I know of right now who is the most sexually active pervert I've ever seen in my life, they want to marry a virgin! When I think about that boy and him wanting to marry a virgin, I think, *Good luck finding one, you little hypocrite!*

There's nothing new under the sun. All these kids now are running around screwing everybody! But, when it comes time to get married, they want clean; they want a virgin.

The chickens have come home to roost on the Sexual Revolution. That's what I think.

The Pill is what has ruined this country!

It ended the stigma associated with promiscuity. Both women and men lost the art of choosing carefully. Their sexual partners became who was available, not someone they might have wanted to marry according to prior methods and the art of making the careful choice.

Productivity in living is connected to monogamy, love and commitment. If you don't have that, what do you truly have, really? If you don't put the effort into one relationship and you're hopping from one to another, you never building anything of lasting value.

After I got married, my husband I had a horrible argument and I told my mother this or that about it, 'He said this and he said that and I can't believe he said that to me,' blah, blah, blah.

My mother said, 'Stop immediately, I'm not listening to this. You might go home and you might fight for another day or two but you'll kiss and makeup. I'm gonna remember all this stuff and be angry at him, but you don't. If you don't like him today, just stick around, you'll like him, tomorrow. Actually, you'll remember why you fell in love with and married him. You're not gonna love him every day your life. You won't know why you love him some days. But that's two people living together. That's the way it is, you have to adjust and adapt.'

I think there's gotta be a commitment. You gotta get in there. And, if you're living together, it's too easy to walk.

When I see a girl with a bastard child, I think to myself, *There's the fruit of the sexual revolution.* Nearly all the women who work for me have children out of wedlock and are not married.

We took some kids from 'normal', middle and upper middle class families to lunch one day. They excused themselves from the table and went to the bar area. They had credit cards. The girls had credit cards. There was a lot of sexual innuendo, and later, activity, going on. I later learned it hit Facebook that night, before we even got home. The girls put it up. They revealed how they had 'scored' with which boys.

Now, where in the hell are we now? Oh, we are way past the sexual revolution of the 70s and 80s, Lord. What we're seeing today came right out of those women screwing everything that walked. Now, we got a whole generation that for which screwing around and putting it on social media is the thing. Girls exclaim, 'I scored with JoJo; I scored with Billy.' It blows my mind.

Heck, we're in a highly religious community. Abstinence is hammered home to hell and back. And, most of these kids out there you're seeing doing this mess, are religious. There are religious kids from all faiths doing this stuff. All this mess is the offspring of the sexual revolution (that started when I was young).

The sexual revolution is what castrated our men. They didn't want to pursue women any more in the classic way because sex with almost any woman they wanted was everywhere. There was nothing left that was good. There was no respect for the women. The women were screwing droves of men, too, and you started having books and Hollywood movies glorifying those so-called relationships.

Everybody's screwing; nobody has commitment. It backfired. That's my opinion.

That's pussified your men.

They just don't want it. Men are warriors. It may be a damn cockroach for God's sake, but they're gonna kill that son-of-a-bitch. That's a man. But, now, he's not fighting for anything. He has nothing to fight for.

He has nothing to protect. He has lost his primordial purpose!

Even his kids are taken away from him because he didn't marry the girl. His children don't have his name. He has no, legal claim as the state and the mother do.

The women rule and it's good for nobody, particularly the children-- poor little bastards. I'm not being facetious: Poor…little…bastards!

My husband is really good about being the man, being strong, killing the cockroach and at the same time, being very gentle and tender with me because we respect each other. I respect him for being a man; he respects me for being a woman. And we have commitment.

In our relationship, I always came first in the family – before the kids, before anything. That's biblical. Children feel secure when they see mom and dad are secure.

The Scripture states that a man will present his wife to Christ, etc. Well, I don't know how you pull that off, but it is there.

And frankly, as there is in the church, there is a hierarchy in the home. I would not want to be a man. You could not pay me enough money to be a man. But unfortunately, nobody else wants to be a man, either!

Most men do not take it seriously. My husband does! My sons do, too.

Before the sexual revolution and The Pill, we men and women respected each other for what we are: The woman, and the man.

# CHAPTER 3

## The Bastardization of America

### The Global Executive says...

*" This know also, that in the last days perilous times shall come. For men shall be lovers of their own selves, covetous, boasters, proud, blasphemers, disobedient to parents, unthankful, unholy, without natural affection, trucebreakers, false accusers, incontinent, fierce, despisers of those that are good, traitors, heady, high-minded, lovers of pleasures more than lovers of God; Having a form of godliness, but denying the power thereof: from such turn away."* (II Timothy 3:1-5)

*"Former Clinton advisor William Galston sums up the matter this way: you need only do three things in this country to avoid poverty—finish high school, marry before having a child, and marry after the age of 20. Only 8 percent of the families who do this are poor; 79 percent of those who fail to do this are poor."* by James Q. Wilson, see http://www.city-journal.org/html/12_1_why_we.html

"Used to, if you were a young woman and got yourself pregnant, two things happened: (1) You married, or (2) your family moved you out of town to hide the fact you were pregnant.

No one wanted to have a bastard in the family. That was life! It was based on centuries of family pride.

In the mid-20th century, less than 5% of the children were born out of wedlock. Today, it's at least 52%. Think about that. Think about the make-up of our country's families.

52% of the population is strongly correlated to the numbers of people who draw benefits from states' and the federal government.

If you relate that back to the statement by the Clinton Advisor mentioned earlier concerning the three things it takes to be in the top 50% wage earners in America, those kids born out of wedlock, the bastard children, are likely to be low wage earners and dependent on the Medicaid and Welfare programs.

Bastard kids are being born in record numbers and are practically guaranteed minimal, educational and job opportunities, if and when they graduate high school at all, because coming from the single-parent situation, the odds are against them.

Again, from historical data, we know that in America, if you don't do those, three things, you'll be a bottom wage earner.

The first thing you have to do to avoid poverty in the United States is to work.

The second thing is to get a high school education.

The third thing is to get married before having children.

If you don't do any one of those three, as the Clinton advisor said, you will likely be a poverty-level wage earner. It's that simple.

By the way, getting married and having children being one of the factors indicates that marriage and offspring from the marriage, are not only good for people, it's good for a society, too!

You'll have people to tell you money is not everything. Our national data and experience are telling us that while money is not everything, it is important because kids having kids is resulting in their kids being reared in poverty. Money does matter!

Poverty drains government services for which workers in a society are dunned through various taxes: Most notably, income taxes.

It's easy to prevent.

All this mess started with The Pill in the 60s. The Pill gave unmarried women the ability to live like promiscuous men, and many did. Ostensibly, because of The Pill, a woman could have as many sexual partners as she wanted and not have to worry about getting pregnant.

So, why are they getting pregnant, left and right, today? I mean, it's a minimal cost to prevent it. If you can't spend $6 per month to have all the sex with all the people you want, you're pretty cheap. If you don't have the money, the government will give the stuff to you.

What is going on is that the girls are using The Pill to game the benefits programs!

What does that mean for the productive workers in our society? (Income) Tax, tax, tax, tax!

Therefore, much of our damn income taxes go to support the underclass we have developed in this country! This, after we have, to date, spent fifteen to 16,000,000,000,000 on our so-called 'War on Poverty'!

We have more poverty now than before we spent the sixteen trillion dollars. What have we done? Where did that money go?

Jesus said the poor will be with us, always. Well, in His omniscience, he must have been thinking ahead 2,000 years to America because we are making sure of it!

Having all these bastards to rear is going to continue to bring the *net* income of the country down!

Remember, by classical definition that goes back centuries to the things held dear in the DNA of our Western civilization, a bastard is a baby born out of wedlock and without the father's name. For example, John Doe is not married to Suzy Q but fathers her baby, so the baby will be named Bob or Sally Q, etc. (not Bob Doe)

To not have a father's name used to be a disgrace. It was uncalled for.

Understanding of this is no longer in our psyche. You might remember those six, teenage girls in New Jersey who formed themselves into a 'pregnant club.' Remember, they got a homeless man to knock all of them up so they could be pregnant at the same time. These were all teenage girls. Not one of them had any means to support a baby.

(A reader told us of another angle on the primordial desire of a girl to have a baby. The reader said, "I was in a high school hallway one day and overheard one girl tell another that she 'got' pregnant so *she* would have someone to love *her.*")

The very idea of something like that would have never happened in this country when I was growing up.

Our loss of decency and honor, exhibited by those girls and all the other non-classical baloney going on these days, dooms us to the specter of continued increases in the percentage of children being born out of wedlock in this country until we have a full nation of bastards!

Adam Corolla wrote that in 50 years, we'll all be chicks. He's not exactly right. Based on the trends, we won't be chicks, we'll be bastard chicks!

Bastards are far more likely to have bastards. The stats show that there is no classic, American Dream for bastards.

Whoever is president of this country cannot sign more income taxes on working and top people of this country into law to the degree needed to yield revenue to pay for all the bastards in this country. There is no more blood in the turnip!

We can only carry so many people! You just can't carry the whole world! You got fewer and fewer makers and more and more takers!

That's the gist of the main problem we have!

Kids are having babies. The mothers are on Medicaid. They deliver at charity hospital or via Medicaid; then, the baby goes on Medicaid and Welfare to the family starts or continues, adjusted for the 'new addition.' In three months (after mother heals up from her most recent pregnancy), she's at it again, getting pregnant! That's the life.

And, talking about poverty in this country, just remember that 85% of poor Americans have color TVs, and 75% have cable service. Our poor are not poor like the poor in the rest of the world. The poor people of the world outside the US would gladly swap places with our poor in the United States!

---

Bastard children are a Latino and black problem, too. Latino unwed births are approximately 72%. Most Latins are Catholics with a moral compass, so to speak. Apparently, the compass is broken!

And, according to blacks and Latinos, they're already discriminated against in society. Why would they want to risk creating further animosity toward them and their families by having illegitimate babies?

Come on, Senor! The child-parents have not finished their educations. They have to drop out of school and take bottom earner jobs. The grandparents become the major caregivers.

Here's a theory for you. Since we workers are paying into government to transfer all this money to all these poor people having bastard children, the governments need to say, 'Girl, if you have one illegitimate baby, we're tying your tubes and administering a vasectomy to the daddy. We're not going to pay for a second baby. You can. We won't.'

In some poor families, the breadwinner of the family is a pregnant mother. Let's be blunt about this. This is serious!

I was reading a story last week about a 14-year-old girl who was pregnant. She rejected an abortion. Her mama told her it was her time to start having babies because they needed the money. She was the third generation.

None of them had ever been married. All the women in this family had been born out of wedlock and had, at their time during the era of social programs that pay the mother to have babies, been the 'breadwinner' for their family (by producing of babies for additional income).

This and other forms government transfer payments to the poor, are going to bleed us to death. Plain and simple: If we don't solve this problem, it's going to destroy our country! We will collapse under the weight of bastard children, 6 pounds at a time!

I suspect it's at the point where it's almost irreversible! There's no stigma to it; no shame, anymore.

On top of that, now we have celebrity women having babies out of wedlock. All the kids are seeing it and thinking it is cool!

Brad Pitt and Angelina Jolie are a good example of Hollywood celebrities having babies out of wedlock and American's middle-class and poor girls looking up to them. Pitt, Jolie and others like them as role models? Baloney!

The girls and who look up to them don't have a pot to piss in. The movie stars seem cool with their bastard babies. It's easy to seem cool and liberal when you got $100 million (and society doesn't have to support you).

And, it seems cool to be a liberal and throw money here and there as Soros does, but he has billions with more being made every day.

Warren Buffett says I should pay more taxes. Well, I don't see Warren writing another check to the IRS. 'Write a check, Warren! I don't see you writing a check. I promise you, the government will take it. Pay more, Warren. It'll make your heart feel better.'

Will he do it? Hell no he won't. Yet, he's going to presume to tell me I need to pay more? Even Soros pays only what he has to.

All these liberals are looking in the wrong direction! The most draining problem we have is the bastardization of America!

This has been growing ever since the 60s. It has now reached critical mass! 52% are bastards! In the US, being a bastard virtually assures you'll be a low wage earner.

Fathers and mothers of the typical bastard child cannot support them. The math doesn't work!

When the government assesses the sperm donor/father for child support, it's based on his earnings and is drawn from his earnings.

The girl/mother gets three or $400 per month.

I know because I employ people. At the time of this writing, I have 40 out of 180 total, male employees from whose pay we must deduct child support payments. None of the deducted, child support payments are over $500- none.

Think about it: The girl/mother gets $300. What does $300 a month do in this economy? $300 won't even pay the rent!!

How is she supposed to buy food, clothing, gasoline, electricity, insurance, etc.?

In addition to the 40 from whom we must deduct per government order, I have 30 to 40 more who voluntarily pay child support obligations. But, if the 30 or 40 ever quit paying, the girl/mothers track them down to me, the employer, and I have to begin deducting and sending it in.

In case you are reading this book and are not an employer of workers, the way it works is that state enforcement services sends me a letter notifying me there is a dead-beat son-of-a-bitch in my employ for whom I must deduct child support payments because his deadbeat butt won't pay it voluntarily!  Clear?

So, I get to do all the bookkeeping, pull the money and send it in (for the mother).

By the way, there are only two or three divorces in the numbers of my employees for whom we are mandated to deduct and who are voluntarily paying the mothers of their children.  The rest are fathers of born illegitimate babies!  Classical bastards!

Get it?  57 or 58 out of 60 have bastard children!

The rules are so messed up that if you're married, you get fewer benefits than parents of the bastards!  What this means is that government programs incentivize living in sin and bastardization!!

Used to be for thousands of years, a woman wanted to mate with the strongest man as though he were the master of a pride of lions-- the strongest lion got to mate, first.  The rest of them took what was left, if anything. That's how a strong gene pool was maintained.

A relatively weaker lion never gets to mate.

Human animals, if you will, used to be that way.

Now, the US government policies are <u>driving weaklings all over the country to procreate</u>!

This is a clue as to why a rich man can always find a woman. It's subconscious but real as Dallas!

The woman doesn't even realize she's making a choice. She doesn't even know why she likes the ugly son-of-a-bitch. Yet, she does.

If the girl's 22 years old, she wants to have a baby. She sees a man, 50 years old with $25 million, or even a wad of $100 bills, and she wants to mate with him because she innately knows that that man, that lion, can take care of her and her baby.

It's not verbalized. It's subconscious.

Why do you think Donald Trump can get all the women he wants? He's an ugly, self-centered, blow hard. But, he's also very rich! So, he will always have a super-model looking wife.

If you analyze it, it's not just the money by itself. This is not politically correct but I'll say it anyway: It's that women 'feel' that the man with the money is smarter.

Frankly, in a way, he is. The cream comes to the top. You can call it what you want. You can excuse it away. But that's the nature of the world. That's the way it works.

You could take the top 10% of this country's wealthiest peoples' money away and in 50 years, they'd have it all back.

Here's the problem now: In the 60s, we started turning our men into pussies. Now, when you talk to women-- and I talked to them all the time --they had just as soon be alone. They don't want to raise the man. They say 'I have two kids. Why would I want another kid?' They don't want to have to support the deadbeat son-of-bitch daddy, too.

Some of these women have a good job. They got an education, got married and divorced because their husband never grew up. He was a kid – he's still a kid –he'll be a kid till he drops dead. That's what women's lib was all about! Women think, 'We're just as strong as the man!'

Well, that's going against DNA of 10 million years! Ten million years, washed away in 50 years in the greatest country, ever! In a snap!

See, millennia ago, men were genetically engineered to be protectors of the hearth and family; and, the strong survived!

Today, we've dumbed the damn country down. We've instituted across-the-board, gender egalitarianism. It's baloney. It's killing us!

We want the schools to take up the slack. I noticed in a report from Florida, that their education authorizes have lowered the scores for respective grades. They didn't raise them. They lowered them so more students could pass and the teachers could keep their jobs.

Of it, a teacher said, 'Well, the tests were unbalanced; unfair.'

Hell, you put the test together, teacher! Now, you didn't teach, you didn't do your damn job and the kids can't pass a test, so you want to dumb the tests down so you won't look like the incompetent fraud you truly are.

In reality, the test was put together by some pinheaded dunce. They lowered the score to get a bigger percentage of kids to pass. They're dumbing down the country!

What we should do is hold teachers responsible! They deserve fair pay but they ought to have to earn it just like I have to earn it.

In my business, if I don't do a good job, I don't get business! If I don't get business, I don't eat.

If you work for me and you don't do your job, were going to send you home! We don't get to lower the minimum score. Those depending on our businesses don't lower our minimum score. We have to perform to keep and grow the businesses!

Performance counts.

But, performance does not count in our educational system. We have probably spent more money on education than any country in the world. Yet, we're 25$^{th}$ in the world. The United States of America, 25$^{th}$ in the world! What?

Back to poor women: They are substituting the state for a man.

They don't want a man but they want a baby. That's what the women's liberation got you! Now, they got it, and they don't like it. And the pussified men say, 'Hey, this is fine with me, I don't have any responsibility.'

That's why we've turned into a bunch of button pushers.

Everybody was talking crazy over this Seal Team Six. Well, they and those like them are exceptions. I'm surprised they found enough men like them to put together a team.

In today's society, fighting, boxing, competitiveness are being watered down. We have football players now who have to be wrapped like furry bunnies. Hell guys, it's football.

Now, they're going to sue because their head hurts. Come on! You loved all the women, money, and various, other accoutrements of your position and status while it was all good.

You knew your head would hurt when you got out there. It's football. You knew what you were signing up for when you wanted to play football. Why should I have to pay for your stupidity?

Well, it's the same thing here, why should I have to pay for the stupidity of these women? Why won't the state regulate the situation instead of incentivizing them?

They regulate everything else. They can regulate these unwed mothers. Regulate illegitimate babies. The government could say, 'If you get married, you can have as many babies as you want and you're gonna take care of them.'

By not educating girls of the data and facts, by not telling these girls, 'Look, if you and the men of your generation don't work, finish high school and get married and have children in wedlock, not out, you are going to guarantee yourself and your children to be crumb snatchers for the rest your life. You are guaranteeing your demise.'

For the boy/man/father, $300 a month for making a mistake is a light penalty, but it's not a killer. He can survive that.

But these girls are in a different boat. It takes $220,000 to raise a child from 1 to 18 years old. That doesn't include a college education.

You divide that by 18 (years): That's over $12,000 a year. She starts off needing $12,000 a year to raise a child and she's getting $300 per month from the daddy, equaling $3600 per year?

She's at least $9,000 a year short before she's paid any rent, or anything!

She and her bastard children go on Medicaid and Welfare and the working people get the bill. Baloney!

# Chapter 4

## How "The Pill" Screwed This Country

## (Yeah, *The* Pill…you know the one!)

*"For the lips of a <u>strange (immoral) woman</u> drop as an honeycomb, and her mouth is smoother than oil: But her end is better as wormwood, sharp as a two-edged sword. Her feet go down to death; her steps take hold on hell. Lest thou shouldest ponder the path of life, her <u>ways are moveable that thou canst not know them</u>…Remove thy way far from her and come not nigh the door of her house.* (Proverbs 5: 3-5, 7-8. King James Bible, underline added)

Helen Gurley Brown was Editor in Chief of Cosmopolitan Magazine from 1965 until 1997. She recently passed away.

Though she pushed Women's Lib, Gurley Brown was not so much like Gloria Steinem and others because Gurley Brown unabashedly loved men and pushed sex. Just before becoming Cosmo's Editor in Chief, she wrote a book, <u>Sex and The Single Girl,</u> which told girls to enjoy sex with many partners, including married men, if and when they wanted.

When The Pill came out, Gurley Brown and Cosmo wrote about it and they stayed behind it from then on (Brown's husband, David Brown, the producer of 'Jaws' and other, famous movies, who wrote the blurbs on the cover of Cosmos for years, wrote the blurb on the cover of her first issue that advertised the article about The Pill).

About The Pill and her first issue of Cosmo, Helen said, "It had a piece about the Pill, which was still new and hadn't really been written about before… To me, the most important thing about it was that if you weren't worried about getting pregnant, you could enjoy yourself more in bed. So we wrote a cover line to that effect… When women saw the line — 'The new pill that makes women more responsive' — they knew *exactly* what Cosmo was talking about and snatched the issue off newsstands in droves."

As we shall see, such a view didn't give a whit about human nature. Such a view has come forward in time. It's ruining Junior High girls and boys.

According to MedIndia.net, actress Raquel Welch, now 71, is of the opinion that the pill has not been good for the institution of marriage in America because it has encouraged promiscuity.

"Ms Welch suggested a 'significant and enduring' effect on women was the idea that they could have sexual intercourse 'without any consequences' with the result that fewer today saw marriage as 'a viable option."

She said she had come to her conclusions after watching what happened to our society's morals and mores over the past 50 years.

The generations of women over the period when Cosmo and other channels began to 'sell' women on the Liberation Movement up to now, have suffered greatly in real, intangible, and profound ways.

The Pill has also continues to generate unsustainable, social and psychological costs.

Thousands of anecdotes could be recorded. Below are two that demonstrate the validity of Ms Welch's opinion.

As a wise woman said years ago, "They are going to go too far."

"They" did.

Who were "They?"

"They" were those in power and Media who pushed the Women's Lib, Sexual Revolution and The Pill to unmarried women and told them they could have sex like, <u>and along with</u>, promiscuous men.

-----

The names and identities have been left out of the following true life stories of American women.

The first is a straight interview told in first person. The second and third are related in the third person.

The first two are daughters of the women who were in their prime when "they " kicked off and push of Women's Liberation, The Sexual Revolution, and The Pill.

The third is a teenager, a "granddaughter" of the revolution.

Truly, within each age (cohort) group, volumes of books could be filled with stories eerily the same as ones below.

Therefore, the following are composites of what has and continues to go on since The Pill and Liberation were introduced.

Put it this way: We heard the "same" stories, over and over.

Human nature is human nature. The Pill makes for predictable, human behavior.

## **Female, 39 years old**

"When I was 14, I got a crush on a boy, a bad boy. It was really stupid, but I was young and I had such a crush on him, I couldn't stand it. He took my virginity-- we were outside in the backyard. How romantic.

I became pregnant from that first encounter. Of course, it was bad for my family. But, we will skip that part because the real thing I want to talk about is The Pill because looking back, it later enabled me to live very promiscuously for a period in my life.

Anyway, the boy was older than I was but he didn't love me so I became a single mother at 14. Of course, this put pressure on my family.

I became pregnant again at 18. This time, it was a little different. The boy was, basically, a good boy. He was going off to the Navy. We had sex for the first and only time before he left and I became pregnant. While he was gone, his family basically turned him against me. So, we did not marry.

After having that baby, I gained a lot of weight and I did not feel attractive. Men did not want me because I was fat. Looking back on it, it affected me psychologically that I was a single mother of two children and men did not find me attractive.

At some point, I got thin, again, looked good, and felt attractive. I did not want to have more babies, so I got on The Pill.

I was surprised to discover that The Pill changed the power: I got the power!

Women got the power (through The Pill). We had the power to have sex or not, and to start f****** like promiscuous men, with promiscuous men.

The Pill changes who you hang out with.

By the way, The Pill did something else: Even before The Pill, women would get pregnant deliberately in order to keep the man. So, with The Pill, women will get pregnant in order to keep him if they want the man, or if they just want a baby from him.

When The Pill came along, the woman could tell a man she was on The Pill, he would trust that, and then she would not take it and get pregnant, on purpose.

The difference is, in that way, the power's with the woman. That is what's going on in much of our society today with the lower income people who are on The Pill-- they get pregnant when they want to by playing the Pill Game.

The Pill did a lot of stuff for women, good and bad.

Back to the social thing, back to women who have babies out of wedlock and have to be supported by the biological father, or the system. It's probably right to say that all women have an innate desire to have a baby, or babies. I mean, women are designed to have babies. It's physiologically obvious!

The desire is there to be a mother. So, what is happening in segments of society is that women, or girls, who are on The Pill, are using it to game the system.

For me, after I lost the weight and felt attractive again, The Pill allowed me to go on a spree, so to speak. Looking back, I was sort of angry. I developed a feeling toward men of, 'Well, you didn't want me when I was fat, now you do; I'm going to do it just because I can, just because I got the power now.'

And, when a woman is on The Pill, particularly if it's a power thing with her, she acts like The Pill is 100%. She does not make a man pull out. That's what the pill is for, in her mind, and she's going to do it naturally, all the way.

I was out there, playing, off and on, for about three or four years. I mean, I was f****** like a playboy. Often, one would call me the next day and I wouldn't have anything to do with them because I was in power then, I controlled the situation. I got my power back from the fat days, and The Pill gave me the authority to do it.

However, over that three or four year period, it wasn't really a constant thing. I would get into a relationship, calm down and have sex with only my boyfriend. In between relationships, I would just do what I wanted to do.

My daddy was a protestant preacher and during this period, I did not really have any guilt about the way I was living. Maybe, eventually down the line, but not while I was doing it.

I felt if promiscuous men do it all the time, I can, too (deep down, I was hurt and mad at them).

They can screw a different woman every night without thinking anything about it. But, we women are different; we take it to heart more than men. We connect more than just sexually. Our emotions are more prone to get involved when we are intimate with someone.

But, during my phase, I cut all that off. I didn't have many emotions about it. I had been hurt so much, I had been through so much, I cut the emotion off. I took The Pill and did it when I wanted to do it and forgot about it.

Early on, The Pill gave me power over men in a certain way, and since I had been hurt so much, I was able to get power back from "men" that had been taken from me, in various ways.

I gave 'em their own medicine.

----------

After my first divorce, I was broken and I went into my chick phase. Here's the thing with girls: the straight up lesbian, they get a so-called straight woman by coming in at their weakest moment, when they know you've been hurt by a man, and all this. They zoom in on that. They do everything just right. They do everything an ideal man would do. They come in; they take care of you; they are attentive-- they really zoom in.

I think my whole sexual life, being out there on The Pill, screwing like a promiscuous man with promiscuous men, getting hurt, then the chick phase because they were more attentive, all of it, was probably started way back to a boyfriend I had – he was married – and I had a big crush on him.

One day we were going to have sex. One of his friend's was over. My boyfriend told me that if I loved him, I would have sex with his friend. I did not want to do it but I felt like I had to do it for him, so I did it. I cried the whole time (Several women readers, some of whom had similar experiences, said this woman, at least at that time in her life, had low self-esteem).

It's one thing to do it when you want to do it. It's completely different when you don't want to do it. <u>That day, my boyfriend took my power.</u>

You see, it wasn't my choice. If I had walked into a room of guys and slept with whoever I wanted to, that would have been from my power. That would have been my choice. But, the guy who made me do it-- he took my power away.

It's like with anything-- if you have a choice, you have the power to choose, or not. But, when someone semi-forces you, they take your power away. It's dehumanizing.

See, the guy put conditions on me. This happens a lot. In my case, he said, 'If you love me.' I did it to please him. My mind was asking, *how can you say you love me, and you are making me do your friend?* In the moment, I felt I did not have a choice in it.

Whether his friend was good-looking, or whether he was someone I would've done on my own, it didn't matter because he presented it, 'If you love me, you cannot do this.'

I knew a girl when I was younger who had a reputation. She liked her guys, sure, but in her way. She had a boyfriend. One day he said, 'Come on over. Me and the guys are going to hang out and watch the ballgame.'

There were nine guys there. He planned the whole thing. He basically ambushed her with an offer when she got there. She wasn't violently raped. She was just in a situation she could not get out of. She had sex with all nine guys, one after the other. And, with her reputation, they acted like she was going along with it, but she wasn't. The boyfriend had taken her power. She was powerless!

Even today, this girl is much older and she's not in a good place because of that incident, long, long ago. She's in counseling, and that's good. But, the point is, when you take away someone's choice, there's no way anything good can come out of it.

Since something similar happen to me, and I'd been hurt along the way by men who lied and cheated on me when we had decided we wouldn't cheat on each other– all sorts of hurts –well, when I got on The Pill, I got my power.

I was doing to them what they had done to me, all along.

Even the chick phase, when the girl came on to me, she did what every man ought to do. In that world, you got studs and femes, studs being the more boyish-- she was a stud. At the time, I was under a lot of pressure, financially, and so forth.

She supported and helped me; we were friends. She came to my house and helped me. She put gas in my car when I needed it. She was my support system. It turned into affection. Before I knew it, we were intimate.

And, here's the thing: a woman knows a woman's body. So, a woman knows what to do to another woman.

And look, when you talk about women thinking they don't need men, you got to talk about the sex toys. When the toys were introduced in this era of, 'We don't need no man,' they multiplied the attitude because, you know, we can turn over and go to the drawer, get satisfaction, put it back in the drawer and go to sleep, all without having to hear or deal with anything coming from a man.

Women don't have to visualize anything to get pleasure when they use a toy. If we want, we can think about an ex-lover; or someone new they want to be with; but, a woman does not have to think about anything or anybody, in order to pleasure herself.

-----

Single motherhood is being glamorized today, too. My girlfriend and I were talking about this, recently.

Celebrities are glamorizing it and the young girls are drinking it up: Single women adopting babies.

This goes back to, 'You don't need a man.' Women like, Charlez Theron and Sandra Bullock, all these stars adopting babies, you know, it's like they're saying, 'You know, I'm single, I don't need a man, I can get a baby, regardless, whether it's through artificial insemination, or adopting, I can get a family, I don't need a man.'

However you cut it, that's what they are doing; that's what they are saying; that is their message. It's showing the world, 'We don't need a man. I'm making money. I always wanted a baby and now I have one. What do I need a man for?' That's the bottom line, pretty much.

But, celebrities doing it is a different thing than a middle-income or poor girl doing it. It's easier to rear a baby when you're making $50 million.

But, the message is the same; so, when the poor girl sees those single women with their babies, she takes the message and has another baby because in *her* economic world, she sees the opportunity for another check and she wrongly assumes she's bringing in more net income.

She thinks, *The government can take care of me and my baby (*as a provider man would*)*.

I hate to say it but that is what is going on!

And, I don't know the data, but I suspect, what I see, is that it's not a black or white thing; it's not along distinct racial lines; it's across the board.

You can talk to people who employ people, who write their paychecks and know about their lives. They know, they say, it cuts across the black and the white races, Hispanics, too.

The mentality is, 'If I have another baby, I can get another check, whether it's from the guy, or from the government. I'm going to be able to take care of it, because somebody's got to take care of me.'

And, it is intergenerational. Grandmother did it. Mother did it. Daughter does it. If the grandmother or the Mama don't break the cycle, it carries on.

That's why I'm so proud. My oldest daughter is 20. I got her to 20 without her having a baby because you know, I was 14 (when I became pregnant with her).

In addition to my 20 year old, I have an 11 and 12 year-old. I have two more to go. I do not want them to repeat my cycle.

I want them to have an education. I want them to have a man who loves them for who they are, a man who can contribute to them.

I want to break the cycle. I want my daughters to do better. I'm fortunate my life has turned out Ok, given the risks I took.

The remark by the Clinton Advisor about the factors that result in poverty, it's true, obviously, because they looked back at data and they revealed the truth of what had happened, over a long time period.

Even though I did what I did at 14, I knew it wasn't right.

There were 10 of us children. I had older sisters who did not do what I did. I could see what they did, how they lived, I knew what was right. I was the only one, out of 10, who had a child before the age of 20.

If I had not become pregnant at 14, my life would've been completely different. If I had found a man after I was 20 who loved me and we had married and had a family,...

But, from where I am now, I can't imagine things any differently. I wouldn't trade my experiences, what happened to me, simply because it showed me what I do not want my daughters to go through.

I think that is one of the redeeming things about it, if there is redemption at all.

The bottom line is that the way I lived is dangerous, and it's not the way to go. But I did it. Now, I have to keep my daughters from repeating the cycle.

I remember hearing that my grandparents married at 15. That was the old days. But, they were married and committed at 15, then started having babies. It wasn't that grandmamma was 14, single, and having babies.

My daughters do not know the vivid details of my life. Except, my 20-year-old, we're very close.

So, she knows some things because I've told her. We basically grew up together. She even knows about the lesbian experiences.

She tells me, 'Mama, I don't want a girl.' But, she had a lesbian friend over the other night for dinner.

I told her, 'Just know who you are. Know who you want to be with. You're young; you don't have kids; I want you to get out there and experience life; but, at same time, be smart about it.' And, I told her, whether she wants to be with a girl or guy, I'll love her, regardless.

The way I see it, I kind of set her free. She's in a better place than I was. I think it is because my parents sheltered me so hard.

It was part of the reason I was pregnant at 14. I'm not blaming the whole thing on them. I'm just saying it played in; there is no doubt in my mind.

------

(After having interviewed many women in the 30 to 50 age range, it is interesting how often their stories contain the same elements: Sexual toys use by the women, and porn viewing by the promiscuous men with whom they consorted, were common denominators.)

### **Sexual Toys and Porn**

The previous woman, the next, and all those we interviewed who "life styled" with promiscuous men are prolific users of sex toys.

As the first interviewee said, their use has exploded since and alongside the introduction of the idea that women no longer need men.

Porn: Porn exploded onto the scene alongside the Women's Lib Movement, the Sexual Revolution, and The Pill (through Super 8 film, followed by the VCR technology). Most women we talked to do NOT watch or read porn.

But, the men they have been with did watch porn, and did to them all the things that porn brought to the fore of society and showed them how to do, e.g. anal sex, all forms and things having to do with oral sex, etc.

The following woman said, 'I have never watched porn.'

What is interesting is that her first, full blown, sexual experience, didn't happen until she was in her early 20's.

Further, the man told her to get on the pill and not only did he take her virginity, like the other story of the woman above, he got his friends in on it and they porned her like the movies she had never watched (and, still hasn't to this day).

She was the female cast member in their 'porn flick.'

### **Female, 45**

This woman had been a life-long church girl. She had good, religious, but legalistic parents and an older brother at the same university during her undergraduate, college years.

In college, she lived the sorority life. She drank and partied (no dope, according to her). She was all the guys' little sister-type. She was very pretty. She dated much.

Except for a college date rape when she was so drunk she didn't know or remember, she graduated college a virgin.

She went away to professional school.

Immediately, she got a crush on a senior. He dressed nice, smelled good, and was about to graduate and begin his professional career.

He had an apartment. She lived in a dorm.

She'd hang out and drink with him and his senior, guy classmates, like she had in college. She was enamored with them. They were seniors. She wanted all them to like her.

Being afraid of getting pregnant, she went to a doctor in the big city and got on the pill.

The senior took her (conscience) virginity.

He was masterful at finding and exploiting others' weaknesses.

Her weaknesses included but were not limited to the fact she wanted everyone to like her; she was insecure about herself; she craved attention (of boys in particular); and, she wanted to be in the popular crowd.

She discovered she loved sex.

He and his friends discussed the fact she liked sex as they did and that since she was on The Pill and he was in control of her desires, he just might be able to talk her into having sex with all them and if he could, it would be a free for all, powered by The Pill.

(Promiscuous men care nothing about protecting a woman!)

He sexed her in every, porn way and she let him because she had a crush on him and wanted to make him happy; besides, she thought, she'd waited a long time to have sex and at some level, she felt entitled; plus, she had visions of life together with him after he graduated.

Even before he got all his buddies involved, he told them everything he did to her, along the way, as it happened.

He and all the guys were at least seven years older than she.

When he was ready and he felt he had her ready, he made the offer as the Serpent offered the apple to Eve.

As the woman in the previous interview whose boyfriend set her up to have sex with his friend, she wanted him to love her.

She acquiesced.

According to her, she did NOT sleep with all them at one time in a gang bang, nor one after the other in the same session; rather, she began to sleep with them on days that were, essentially, covertly scheduled by 'her boyfriend' and his posse of promiscuous men/boys.

Generally, it all happened in his apartment. His roommate, and others who were there on any occasion, could hear the action through the door, walls, and heating and air conditioning vents. She knew they all listened in because it was common sense and because her boyfriend and they blatantly told her so. But, she was powerless to do anything about it.

He had taken her power.

His plan could not have worked without The Pill because it freed all the men from consequences!

Just as he'd planned, he had made her 'one of the promiscuous guys'.

Behind her back, they called her their little nympho!

Her poor daddy and mother were back in her small town, completely unaware their daughter had become the sexual pawn to a group of older, promiscuous men.

She would go to her Protestant church every Sunday then go over to his apartment, or one of theirs, and have sex in the afternoon. Her boyfriend always had first right of refusal.

Her power having been taken, she would hang around with them, drinking and watching sports, etc., and in front of her and by her acquiescence, all her promiscuous, sexual colleagues talked openly about f****** her.

All she could do was laugh and say, "Well, I didn't know what I was missing; yes, I like sex, what's wrong with that?"

She was liberated, and trapped all at the same time!

If the pill had failed and she had become pregnant, multiple, paternity tests would have been needed in order for her to avoid being alone in the struggles that would have come.

After the situation with her boyfriend and his posse ran its course, the guys graduated and they married the girls, the women, they had been taking to dinner, on proper dates, while they were having marathon sex with her when she was, promiscuously, in their posse of promiscuous men.

Her reputation was ruined at school and in her professional community (in that city).

She said that in addition to everything, they lied about her. It is hard to imagine what they lied about. Maybe they said she had sex with more than one of them at a time, in some manner and combination.

According to her, she didn't do it. She said, "I was not a whore."

About the scandalous thing blew up and the word got out, she said, "It wasn't like that," probably because she had a different, psychological view of the thing. For example, she said, "They liked me."

Perhaps, in her mind, she was correct.

In her mind, he was her boyfriend. She was doing all the others, for him.

The Pill created for her, and thousands of other girls and women, an extreme moral hazard, along with untold risks!

What she was saying, too, was that she had done it because her boyfriend wanted her to do it, and she was desperate for him to love her and she wanted to make him happy: She wanted him to be pleased with her.

These feelings are of the primordial natures of women and men. In removing the primary goal and consequences of sex, The Pill makes way for the fallen nature of man (and woman) to run loose after its own desires.

He had figured out her weak points and keyed on them, then porned her out and to his friends under at least one guise: That they liked her and wanted her in their 'posse,' contingent on certain things.

For reasons beyond our scope, he received extra pleasure by orchestrating his and his friends' opportunity to hear the sounds of her passion run amok, through the door, walls, and vents.

And, finally, he made her take the blame (onto herself).

She says, "I didn't do everything they said I did. But, I did do it. It was the dumbest thing I ever did. I should have never gone along with that. There is not a day that goes by that I don't wish I hadn't."

----

After that, she went on a spree to get a man to love her.

She met the next man at a fancy bar. He was on a date with another girl but boldly walked over, got her number and called her later. They started sleeping together because sex had become the dominating thing of her relationship with men.

She said they never talked about if they were free to sleep with others. She had no power. She couldn't tell him what to do. She finally caught him in bed with the girl with whom he was on a date the night he met her at the fancy bar.

He was a second generation, rich brat. She said she was always the girl he wanted around when he had a party at his house on the water. To think that way about it made her feel more special than the other girls she could see circulating in his world.

There was always much alcohol. He was a cocaine head, but never in front of her.

Her first boyfriend, his posse, and the subsequent, rich brat, and every one after that over seven years, except for one man, did drugs, never around her, but always before she arrived or otherwise, behind her back.

Being stoned apparently heightened their sexual pleasure. She drank.

She was liberated and suffered love addiction, enabled by The Pill.

None of the men in the first posse, nor any after, ever apologized because she had been a promiscuous man, along with them.

----

Two, interesting things came out of her first experiences. Things Helen Gurley Brown, et al, gave not a twit about: She developed a warped sense of the good side of jealousy.

To wit, she was taught to ignore what the first, promiscuous men in 'her' posse did on the outside as she tried everything to get the central boyfriend to love her because he, and they, had taken her power and her right to be jealous of any woman, or to demand anything of them, because they didn't demand anything of each other, and she was one of them, a promiscuous man, and on The Pill. It was a free for all, skewed in their favor!

Those guys were simultaneously dating girls-- so called good girls, girls they were taking to dinner and for whom they were buying flowers and would later marry —while they explicitly told her, and demonstrated that their lives outside their sex ring were none of her damn business.

Of course, the experts would say it didn't matter: "She was liberated." She was on The Pill.

After several men, and after she figured out the game of the life with promiscuous men she would lead for several more years, she got her legs, as it were, and began to 'give it back to them.'

Other women, including the woman in the previous interview, referred to this phase as the, 'I started to f*** back' phase. This woman called it that, too, in similar words.

Instead of learning and stopping or demanding boundaries that would increase her odds of finding true love, marriage, and children-- the things women like her now acknowledge are the things for which they are naturally geared and wanted --she escalated her numbers and the intensity of sexual encounters.

She tore into the bar life in the 90's, even while she looked like a church girl and continued to be 'active' in her big, Protestant church.

She was good in her profession.

At the party period's zenith and in various ways, as she continued to have sex like a promiscuous man with promiscuous men for pleasure and as a means to get her power back, she said she often felt like screaming, "Can't someone see this empty finger. Someone stand up and put a ring on it!"

If you don't think this story is typical, you don't know what is going on!

The point again is, she could not have lived the life she lived without The Pill.

Her lifestyle was very risky in many, physical ways and very costly on emotional and spiritual levels.

She finally married a wealthy man after he made her sleep with him for two years. He proposed marriage, just in time, because she had begun to think he did not want her and that she was going to have to leave him. She stayed married for 14 years, had at least 2 affairs her husband didn't know about, and now, she's divorced.

When and if she talks about grad school and the promiscuous man who took every inch of her virginity then shared her with his classmates, she speaks only of him, as though the others didn't exist.

### The next generation: 17 years old

We interviewed scores of teens and they all had similar stories.

There was one we decided to relate because the girl was particularly sage for her age.

She told us she is almost 17 years old.

She said she is still a virgin.

She said that boys these days have sex on their minds, all the time. She said easy girls are everywhere and giving sex to the boys.

She said that as a result, virginity in her age group is very rare. Consequently, she said, getting married a virgin is almost unheard of.

She told us that being a virgin has become a technical designation. Many girls in her age group are doing other, sexual things in order to 'keep their virginity' (we leave it to the reader to fill in the blanks).

She has a good boyfriend. They have had no form of sex. She said he is the first boy to ever open a door for her—any door—car; entrance to a restaurant; any door.

She said something interesting: Most boys expect a girl (and they say it) to be "their bitch."

She said that before her current boyfriend, she had boys try things on her but that she never let them do anything. She said that these days, in her age group, girls are too easy!

This young lady attends an exclusive, private school. She said that 70 to 80% of the girls in her grade, she's a junior, are on The Pill!

Further, all the girls on The Pill are having sex; and, there are even more who are not on The Pill but having sex, anyway.

She said something we heard from other aged women: There is a feeling among girls that once you've had sex, it no longer matters. Therefore, she knows of girls in her grade who, since losing their virginity, have had sex with fifteen to 20 guys.

She said she was being serious, that some lost count after they ran out of fingers. She said some of the girls lost their virginity in the eighth grade.

She said her observation is that many girls do not respect themselves. She said that after they lose their virginity, they always have sex when they go out on a date, that it is part of the date. .

She said she feels the media promote it is perfectly normal to have sex all the time; that nobody has morals anymore; that nobody really cares; that most no longer give a damn.

She pointed out that guys, men, reach their peak early, at 18, 19 and 20. But, women reach theirs in their 30's. She mused that it seemed weird that 16 year old girls were having all this sex with all these boys. She said demonstrated their lack of self-respect.

She also pointed out that it is the mothers of the 16, 17 year olds on The Pill who got them on it. She said that in her age group, when a mother knows her daughter is having sex, the mothers don't want them to get pregnant so they get them on The Pill. She called that a lack of leadership (Author's comment: Their mothers are $2^{nd}$ generation, Cosmo girls, themselves).

She said she is even aware of a handful of girls in the $7^{th}$ and $8^{th}$ grades who have lost their virginity.

Putting what's going on in a larger, national perspective, she pointed out she knows someone who works at the local hospital in the baby center. She said that recently, 8 out of 10 of the babies in there were of single mothers who did not know who was the father. She said, "That's where we are."

She shifted gears and said that in spite of all the facts, she does not know a girl who doesn't want a guy to respect her. She said girls want to be respected, that they want to be treated as a princess. They want to be put on a pedestal.

At the same time, she said the girls want guys to like them and that's a problem because in high school, if you are a whore, or if you're sleeping with a boy, the word gets around and you'll have guys all over you. She said the girls mistake that for being liked (in a wholesome way).

The girls, she said, give away their self respect, their self esteem, to be liked.

She said that of course, it doesn't work. A perplexed look crossed her face and she said it's a paradox that girls want guys to respect them, yet they don't respect themselves.

She speculated it had to do with family. She pointed out that her extended family is involved in her life. Her mother and father, individually and together as husband and wife, are involved in her life. She intimated what the executive's wife said: the element of family being tightly knit, or not, made a big difference.

She admitted it would be easy to fall into temptation. She said that what she does to offset the risks is to stay focused on the pros, the life positives, of staying on the right path.

She said she has locked in on the fact that keeping oneself a (true) virgin until married and waiting to be married before having children (virginity takes care of that), makes life easier on a girl.

She said that she understands life is difficult for everyone. Therefore, her staying locked on the positives is her way to keep like as good as it can be; her way of not making it worse by being foolish.

She says that girls need to wait on that one guy who really loves them and that they love. She said that will help assure life will be better.

She said she does not know why more girls don't stay focused on the good things. She said she suspects that they have come to believe there are no good guys left; and, that they want to be popular, immediately, at any cost; and, they want guys to like them.

She said she feels fortunate, maybe even lucky, to have her boyfriend. She said, he's a good guy who cares for her, that she never feels there are conditions to his admiration of her.

She said he's rare. She said there are not many like him. She reiterated that girls think, "Oh well, I'll just give him what he wants and maybe he'll love me. She said, that is their low self-esteem coming out.

She said she thought deeply and knows this: The girls who give themselves to bad guys actually think in their hearts and minds that the guys are going love them because they gave it to them. They think that even though he's a jerk at first, he's going to change (after they give him what he wants).

She said she tells them, "You can't change a man. You might change what he wears but you can't change him!"

She said that why, when a guy cheats on a girl, he'll do it, again. She said that when a girl goes back to a cheater after he's cheated on her, she's making a big mistake. She told us she has girls coming to cry on her shoulder all the time. When they go back to the cheating guy, she tells them, "Are you crazy? He's not going to change."

She told us that only thirteen percent of the senior girls have not had sex (conversely, 87 percent have). She said she is close friends with one of the senior virgins and she tells her the senior girls who have had sex say, "Oh it's so good, why haven't you done it?" She said, that's what we've come to.

She told us it is clear that it matters who you hang around with. She has several friends with whom she is close. All are true virgins. None have done any extra-intercourse things.

She said it helps all them to be friends.

She told us that she went through the yearbook one time and checked the girls who had NOT had sex. They were approximately 10%.

She reiterated that 80% of the girls in her class are on The Pill. She astutely identified a critical nuance about the mothers having put their daughters on The Pill.

(Note what The Executive's Wife said about The Art of Choosing):

*"Back in my day, you did not have sex with someone who would not be responsible. In other words, if you were going to have sex, you were going to pick someone, decide to have sex with someone who you knew would be responsible. It was instinctual. Instinctively, you knew you had to pick somebody who was going to take care of you and the baby. This was important before THE PILL because you had no out. Sex had consequences. Back then, when I was young and really wanting to have sex like any other human, they were lined up outside my door, so to speak, I had to know that the man was a good man would care for me and the baby if we got pregnant because there was NO PILL, no out. We have lost the 'Art of Choosing.'*

The girl intuitively noticed the distinction between the two era's methods of avoiding the consequences of pre-marital sex. She said, "Nowadays, there's an out for everything. We have a pill for sex and every other thing we want to get out of. Where are our morals? We don't have any. That's what's wrong with our generation, and the generation ahead of us."

She said, she feels people no longer really believe in God. She said she has a close relationship with Him. She said that relationship helps.

The thought of God made her comment: "You know, the thing about my boyfriend is that I know he cares for my soul. What this means is that if we did have sex and I did become pregnant, I know he'd be there for the rest of our lives. We're not going to have sex. We've decided that. I'm only saying this to say that almost all boys today no longer care for the souls of girls. They only care about how they look. They only care about their bodies. They don't love. They don't care about the girl inside."

She wisely said that if you talk to older women who were in high school 50 years ago, there's a viewpoint they had that has been lost. She said, "It was that they intuitively knew, probably because they did not have The Pill as backup, that if they were going to have sex, they knew to choose someone they knew would take care of them and their baby if they became pregnant."

She said, "Girls today are jumping out of the proverbial airplane and into sex every day because they have what they think is a parachute, The Pill. They are not factoring in the damage to their self-esteem and self-worth, or potential, mental anguish and guilt, later."

# Chapter 5

## The Cosmos Girl, Now!

The post-modern Cosmo Girl of today is in middle-school, or younger!

In <u>Aggressive Girls, Clueless Boys</u> (Family Life Publishing, 2012), Dennis Rainey brings to light a problem that is almost out of control and touches all parents and families with boys and girls. He writes on page 4 about the shift in our country: "Sex among teenagers is old news, unfortunately, as is aggressive boys pursuing girls, men pursuing women, and adult women pursuing adult men. But a growing number of parents…are learning that something has shifted in our culture over the last couple of decades. Increasingly, girls are aggressively (sexually) pursuing boys-- in high school, middle school, and even earlier –in numbers we never saw in the past. The rules have changed, and many parents are asking for help in how to protect their young sons. This shift has caught them by surprise, and they don't know what to do." (Parenthetical added)

Examples abound in Dennis' book. "My ten-year-old son was enticed by another fifth grade girl via e-mail to open another e-mail account so that I couldn't monitor it. But I found it and cancelled it. She is sending e-mail messages and e-cards to him and two of his friends in a love quadrangle that she's brilliantly orchestrated."

A principle at a Christian school told Dennis Rainey of something prevalent in schools…"a combination of sexual aggression and cyber-bullying. He shared how girls are texting boys, often in the middle of the night, and pushing them to 'grind' with them (imitating sex with their clothes on) or pay the price of ridicule and rumor."

Rainey makes it clear aggressive boys are still out there doing damage. He doesn't excuse them or their behavior.

However, the problem with aggressive girls has become so powerful and wide spread, it deserves its own coverage, and parents with young boys need to be preparing themselves, and their boys.

He gives reasons for this phenomenon:

"A growing number of children are growing up <u>without the positive influence of an intact marriage</u> (underline added). With our high rate of divorce and out-or-wedlock births, we have a generation of sons and daughters who hardly know their fathers or who are forced to split their time between mom's house and dad's. The only time they see their parents interact is when they are arguing over money, visitation schedules, or their new girlfriend or boyfriend. These children never see a healthy model of a male-female relationship. Many boys are not shown or taught what it means to be a man. And without even realizing it, girls seek to fill their need for male love, attention, and affirmation by preying upon these unsuspecting and curious boys."

Then, without calling it so, and probably not realizing the provenance of the situation, he attributes the phenomenon to the manifestation of the new, what we call, "Middle-School Cosmo Girl"™:

"Much more than in the past, girls are exhorted to be aggressive in all areas of their lives. It is one thing to encourage girls to excel and pursue their dreams. The problem is encouraging a *lifestyle of aggression*-- doing whatever it takes to get what they want, no matter who they hurt—especially using their sexuality to exert power over men."

He's writing this book to serious minded, Christian parents who are concerned and committed to guard their children and deliver them, as unmolested as possible by evil in the world, into a solid adulthood full of positive relationships.

So, he writes:

"Many parents pull away too quickly from their children. Parenting feels much easier when your children are in the relatively easy years of ages five through eleven. This is a time when they want to spend time with you, they listen to you, and they think you are wise. But as those same children enter adolescence, they begin acting more independently. They want to spend more time with their friends than with you. They argue with you more frequently and question your wisdom…and sanity. Some of this is normal. Children *need* to become independent and to grow up. And that means that their relationship with their parents will change. But you cannot-- you must not --pull away from them. Not now, not yet. Not in one of the most vulnerable seasons they will face."

He and some of the serious minded parents he quotes in his book, who have been surprised by what they have seen from The Post Modern, Middle School Cosmo Girl™, likely do not fully realize who they are dealing with:

She is the granddaughter and daughter of two Cosmo girls before her, both of whom are shallow and worldly in a bad way and the daughter of a weak father, for whose attention and affection she has craved for years. And, statistically, mother and father are probably divorced and divorced or not, he and she are more concerned about living their lives, 'in the full,' than demonstrating to and rearing her for a loving, fulfilling relationship with a man.

# Chapter 6

## Men Who Won't Protect and Provide for Their Wives and Families

*"But if any one does not provide for his own, and specially for those of his house, he has denied the faith, and is worse than the unbeliever."*
(1 Tim 5:8, Darby Bible Translation)

----

*The Decline of Man:*

*Non working men: Since 1950, the number of non-working men (unemployed, imprisoned or disabled) has increased from 5% to 30%.*

*Earnings: Women's earnings grew 44% between 1970 and 2007, while men's only grew 6%.*

*Out-of-wedlock births: At the same time, the number of fatherless children has increased from 11% in 1970 to 27% in 2010, with a total of 40% of births being out-of-wedlock.*

*Religious interest: The religious interest of men has also dropped with only 39% of men attending church regularly.*

*Time playing video games: Meanwhile, 18-34 year old men spend more time playing video games daily than the typical 12-17 year old boy.*

*Source: cnn.com, 10/4/11 as reported by the AFA Journal, February 2012.*

--------

The pussification of the American male not only ruined him morally, it robbed him of his pride and volition to provide for his family.

The following is a true story from a real, American woman. We interviewed many more and could fill volumes with stories just like this.

Interestingly, the same elements appear in every story. It's almost eerie. You know one pussified male, you know 'em all!

Hence, the following is a composite of droves of women who have had, essentially, the same experience.

----

"I'm 46 years old.

I was married for 10 years to a highly self-centered man. It took quite a while for me to realize just how self centered he was.

Actually, we dated for seven years and he acted normally during that whole time. It was only after we got married, immediately after we get married, as in we were in the car on the way back from having just been married, did he drastically have not been good and are not of the sort to lead to love, respect and marriage.

We were talking about this earlier today. She told me she gets lots of responses and that they always seem so nice. The men say they are looking for ordinary friendship; a good, outgoing woman, blah, blah, blah.

Recently, after talking with a prospective man only a few times, the next thing she knew, the guy sends her a picture of his pecker!

What the hell is that? She says there are more of those than not. I think there's something wrong with somebody, anybody, who will take a picture of himself and put it out for the world to view. What is that about?

Everybody has lost morals.

Another thing is happening is women with women. You wouldn't call it lesbianism; they just call and having fun. I know the younger generation calls it just having fun. I think we are a generation or two into the Sexual Revolution and its gone crazy…chickens home to roost.

I have a friend my age who is a beautiful girl. My sister and I found out gender does not matter to her because we went out with her one night and she said, 'If there aren't any guys here, there are a lot of pretty girls. Either way it goes, I'm not going to be by myself tonight.' She's typical.

From what I can tell, that type stuff goes back to the entertainment aspect of it. Many people are using sex for entertainment. I think they are losing out. They don't see it that way.

By losing out, I mean that when you look to sex for entertainment, there is no real connection; there can be no valuable emotion; no real anything. It's just entertainment.

We used to believe God didn't make it for that.

Men and women my age say that in dating, they are after real connection. And, in a way, they think they are going to find it.

However, many I know always have their foot in the door somewhere else because they are afraid of being alone; they always leave other doors open in case things don't work out in any, one situation.

They don't focus on the good they have, when and if they have it.

They play the negative games with several at a time. That's what I'm saying. They have simultaneous, unhealthy relationships, often based on sex and each other trying to get control.

In the end, they end up by themselves-- their worst fear ends up being realized. This happens to men and women.

Decades ago, the men started getting frustrated. They became unfocused. Heck, I've been watching that happen over my years.

Women, including myself, started thinking they could do it themselves. After that, they starting thinking they could do it *all* themselves– be the boss of the house, so to speak. You know, burn the bra with a new twist. 'We can do everything by ourselves – we don't need no stinking man.' Women wanted men when they wanted them, every now and then, but they decided they didn't really need them at all.

The minute that attitude concreted up, the men got lazy about everything.

The more the years went on, the more the women decided they could do for themselves. The men got lazier, and lazier. Now, the roles are swapped.

Now, the men want to be at home and let the women take care of them. I kid you not!

Some women are Ok with that. But, the majority of women are saying it's harder and harder to do that for many reasons, including that it's tough to make it in the economy, especially now.

In addition to bringing home the bacon and all that, women still have the home to take care of because the desire to nest and take care of her home is in the woman's makeup. Also, it's in the woman's DNA to take care of her children. That's just the way it is. It's ridiculous to deny it.

The women have created the pussified men of today. As a result of what the women have enabled, the women have to be men and now they resent it. The error has come full circle. Now, women resent men.

In a way, the powers that drove the idea and enticed women into the Sexual Revolution, are the ones who did us all in. It is clear that women should have never fallen for it hook, line and sinker; and, that their falling for it hurt them and has, over the decades, ruined the American male.

On the economics side of things, women have to worry if a man who is after them can make a living.

You don't have to listen too hard today to hear that men are interested if the woman can make a living. The wussy men want a big paycheck from the woman. That's their goal.

You can clearly see it. When I meet a new man, the things he wants to know, right up front, are my name; what I you for a living and where I work; and, where I live. That's it.

Think about this: What they are doing is from 'what you do' and 'where you live,' they are making all sorts of economic deductions, deductions which determine if they want to continue with the conversation, or not. The funny thing is that they could be missing out because those things are not indicative of everything of value about a woman. And, if the man was a strong provider and had a damn work ethic, he wouldn't care about where the woman lives, what she does, and how much money she makes.

In our part of the country, the men like women who work in medical and other fields who have a decent, good or high salary because if they can get a woman who makes a good check, they can take off a little more; work a little less, and it will be all right.

Ironically, this circles back to the point that women who have to work a lot because they have to be the man, are not as able as they need to be, to help mold their sons into the men they ought to be when they grow up.

Consequently, sons of weak fathers grow up with no true respect for women because their rearing on matters of healthy, men and women relationships was weaker than it should have been. You don't have to be a PhD to see that this has to be one of the main reasons this wussified men thing goes inter-generational, and is getting worse.

For example, I have a 10-year-old son from a man I could no longer be married to because he turned out to fail in the ways we are talking about. When we met and dated, I had a big job in the medical field. It came out (years) later that he chased me because he wanted to look big in front of his friends. It was all about, 'My wife does this,' and 'This is where we live,' etc.

After we divorced, he was supposed to have our son on the weekends. But, most of the time he goes fishing by himself, or with his buddies. Much of the time, he doesn't work because he doesn't really want to.

In the meantime, he's proud 'about' his son; not necessarily 'of' his son. There is a difference.

He says out loud, 'That's my boy.' Every time our son does something good, he is quick to say, 'That's my boy. I'm so proud; my boy can fish; my boy can hunt; my boy can do this or that.'

We got into a fuss yesterday. His 'pride' statement came up in response to something our son did. He said, 'I'm proud of my boy.'

I responded, 'You damn well ought to be: Mama brings home the bacon; puts a roof over our son's head; puts food in his stomach. Again, I am the one who is teaching your boy how to be a man: I taught him how to run the lawnmower; I taught him how to fix his bike; I taught him how to fish; I have taught and continue to teach him how to be a man. I did all that. Mama did that. Not you.'

'You are too busy laying up on your ass trying to be *your* daddy's little boy-- fishin' and huntin' and all that with him instead of with *your* son. You need to be the one taking your son fishing, not me. You need to be the one finding him a good place to go hunting this fall, not me.'

'But, Mama does all that! That stuff is what I do for our son. Your son and I go hunting. Your son and I go fishing. We work on the house and keep it in good shape. I am the one who has taught him about all the tools and we have learned how to use them to keep things fixed. I do that—M A M A does all you should be doing. And then you have the gaul to say you are so proud of him! You should be. And, you can thank ME!'

'I did it and I'm doing it!'

Ex-husband will never have a marriage to work because he doesn't really work after he settles into a marriage. He finds a way to weasel out of it. Now, when he meets his 'next wife,' he always has a good job. But, eventually it slacks off.

When we met, I had a great job and a nice place to live. It came out later that when he met me, he thought, *Oh, I'm going to hook up with her*. Then, after we got married, he got hurt at work and didn't work for two years, but he could have. When he finally did go back to work, it was hit and miss but again, I know for a fact that he was not legitimately hurt.

When all that happened, I had the children to rear and another, bigger child: My husband! I took care of him while he piled up on the couch watching Direct TV that I was paying for, while he waited on me to fix his supper.

That's it. That's all he did, except for running around with his friends, when he wanted. Later, he couldn't imagine why the relationship didn't work.

So basically, the way he operates is that when he's not married, he'll get a good job and it'll look all good because he is an electrician and can make money. From there, he'll attract, or target a woman who has a good job and at some point, he'll get her to marry him.

It goes downhill from there in ways it went downhill with us. This scenario happens over and over. He is perpetually worthless.

I got tired of it. All of his new wives get tired of it, some quicker than others.

Most women today really want a man to man up. The women are tired, really.

No matter what she says she wants or what she does, she is fed up with pussified men and is ready for one to man up.

Women today want their own liberty to do and go, sure, but they want a partner as well. They want a man to help bring it together and make things work.

Women are looking for partnership. They're really looking for someone to come in and take care of them."

----

Another woman reader, approximately 34 years old, told what women want:

"We want someone to support and grow us in what we do; someone to help us become better persons; someone with whom we give and receive support for what the other does (for earning a living)."

Chapter 7

# STATE FUNDED POVERTY IS GOING TO KILL US!

## Medicaid and Welfare

*"If something is unsustainable, that means it won't be sustained."* The late Herbert Stein, Chairman of the Council of Economic Advisors for Presidents Nixon and Ford.

*"For even when we were with you, this we commanded you, that if any would not work, neither should he eat."* (2 Thess. 3:10, King James Bible)

Poor people use your state's Medicaid for medical coverage to deliver and medically care for bastard children (and, they use Welfare for income).

Sure, Medicaid has legitimate functions but that's not what this book is about.

This book is about, in part, the moral failure of this country and how workers/Federal Income Tax payers are being used to support irresponsibilities of others.

Any worthwhile and responsible analysis of the pussification of our country and the risks of financial failure going forward, must inform that the one thing that could break your state where you live is medical costs for the poor: Medicaid.

Long before Obama Care, the flags were going up.

On study in particular stands out: In their pivotal study done several years ago titled, "State and Local Finance: Increasing Focus on Fiscal Sustainability", Robert B. Ward and Lucy Dadayan concluded "...Medicaid...became the single largest threat to state/local fiscal sustainability." This study can be downloaded from http://publius.oxfordjournals.org/

What does Medicaid costs have to do with The Pussification of America? The abuse of The Pill and the costs to Medicaid for childbirth; the subsequent insurance of mother and children; and, the perceived financial incentive to have babies created by other forms of state aid to Medicaid beneficiaries (which drives gaming the systems and taxpayers by beneficiaries), throw gas on Medicaid costs that were already unsustainable.

### Why the Increase in Bastards?

"Former Clinton advisor William Galston sums up the matter this way: you need only do three things in this country to avoid poverty—finish high school, marry before having a child, and marry after the age of 20. Only 8 percent of the families who do this are poor; 79 percent of those who fail to do this are poor.

This pattern of children being raised by single parents is now a leading feature of the social life of almost all English-speaking countries and some European ones. The illegitimacy ratio in the late 1990s was 33 percent for the United States, 31 percent for Canada, and 38 percent for the United Kingdom.

Now, not all children born out of wedlock are raised by a single mother. Some, especially in Sweden, are raised by a man and woman who, though living together, are not married; others are raised by a mother who gets married shortly after the birth. Nevertheless, there has been a sharp increase in children who are not only born out of wedlock but are raised without a father. In the United States, the percentage of children living with an unmarried mother has tripled since 1960 and more than doubled since 1970. In England, 22 percent of all children under the age of 16 are living with only one parent, a rate three times higher than in 1971.

Why has this happened? There are two possible explanations to consider: money and culture.

Money readily comes to mind. If a welfare system pays unmarried mothers enough to have their own apartment, some women will prefer babies to husbands. When government subsidizes something, we get more of it. But for many years, American scholars discounted this possibility. Since the amount of welfare paid per mother had declined in inflation-adjusted terms, and since the amount paid in each state showed no correlation with each state's illegitimacy rate, surely money could not have caused the increase in out-of-wedlock births.

This view dominated scholarly discussions until the 1990s. But there are three arguments against it. First, the inflation-adjusted value of welfare benefits was not the key factor. What counted was the inflation-adjusted value of *all* the benefits an unmarried mother might receive—not only welfare, but also food stamps, public housing, and Medicaid. By adding these in, <u>welfare kept up with inflation</u>. (Underline added)

Second, what counted was not how much money each state paid out, but how much it paid compared with the cost of living in that state. As Charles Murray pointed out, the benefits for a woman in New Orleans ($654 a month) and those for one in San Francisco ($867 a month) made nearly identical contributions to the cost of living, because in New Orleans it cost about two-thirds as much to live as it did in San Francisco.

Third, comparing single-parent families and average spending levels neglects the real issue: how attractive is welfare to a low-income unmarried woman in a given locality? When economist Mark Rosenzweig asked this question of women who are part of the National Longitudinal Survey of Youth—a panel study of people that has been going on since 1979—<u>he found that a 10 percent increase in welfare benefits made the chances that a poor young woman would have a baby out of wedlock</u>

<u>before the age of 22 go up by 12 percent. And this was true for whites as well as blacks</u>. Soon other scholars were confirming Rosenzweig's findings. Welfare made a difference. (Underline added)

But how big a difference? AFDC began in 1935, but by 1960 only 4 percent of the children getting welfare had a mother who had never been married; the rest had mothers who were widows or had been separated from their husbands. By 1996 that had changed dramatically: <u>now approximately two-thirds of welfare children had an unmarried mom, and hardly any were the offspring of widows</u>. (Underline added)

Why this change? ....

...To explain the staggering increase in unmarried mothers, we must turn to culture. In this context, what I mean by culture is simply that being an unmarried mother and living on welfare <u>has lost its stigma</u>. At one time living on the dole was shameful; now it is much less so. As this may not be obvious to some people, let me add some facts that will support it. (Underline added)

Women in rural communities who go on welfare leave it much sooner than the same kind of women who take welfare in big cities, and this is true for both whites and blacks and regardless of the size of their families. The studies that show this outcome offer a simple explanation for it. In a small town, everyone knows who is on welfare, and welfare recipients do not have many friends in the same situation with whom they can associate. But in a big city, welfare recipients are not known to everyone, and each one can easily associate with other women living the same way. In the small town, welfare recipients tell interviewers the same story: 'I always felt like I was being watched'; 'they treat us like welfare cattle'; people 'make nasty comments.' But in a big city, recipients had a different story: Everyone 'is in the same boat I am'; people 'don't look down on you.'

American courts have made clear that welfare laws cannot be used to enforce stigma. When Alabama tried in 1960 to deny welfare to an unmarried woman who was living with a man who was not her husband, the U.S. Supreme Court objected. Immorality, it implied, was an outdated notion. The states have no right to limit welfare to a "worthy person," and welfare belongs to the child, not the mother. If the state is concerned about immorality, it will have to rehabilitate the women by other means."

by James Q. Wilson, see http://www.city-journal.org/html/12_1_why_we.html

# Chapter 8

## Middle Eastern and World Oil is Bleeding Us Dry!

## (How We Lost the Initial Battle for Oil, Then the War)

### The Executive Says…

"In case you've never heard of a man named Armand Hammer, here's how our unnecessary dependence on Middle Eastern and World Oil began.

Armand Hammer was a man who became rich through trading with Russia.

He entered the oil industry through acquisition of Occidental Petroleum, an oil and natural gas exploration and development company. Occidental was much smaller than the smallest of the big oil companies.

Eighty percent of his small company's production was out of Libya. The seven big oil companies, referred to at that time as 'The Seven Sisters,' also operated in Libya but differently in that their total supply to their businesses was diversified all over the world, not just Libya.

Someone smart and powerful in Libya knew they could not put the squeeze on one of the seven sister companies because the seven sisters, individually and together, would shut down their Libyan operations. Libya was not critical to them.

On the other hand, the Libyans told Hammer, 'We want you to give us our asking price above the current, world price.' Given the fact that 80% of his production came from Libya, Hammer went to the Seven Sisters and asked them to make up his Libyan supply, at their costs, if he told the Libyans no and they cut him off. The Seven Sisters could have easily done it. They said no. Consequently, Hammer caved in to the Libyans.

The Libyans then went to the seven sisters and said 'Hammer is giving us this price and we want it from you, too.'

That is when the upward spiral of oil prices began. The price of oil impacts everyone in our economy. Even if you just grow watermelons, the price of watermelons has to go up because you've got to have fuel to plow the field, etc.; the watermelons have to be trucked, etc., etc.

Everything in this country is tied to the price of transportation.

This is why it is ridiculous to talk about electric cars as if electricity comes down from the heavens in great lightning bolts and fuels everything. Electricity comes from fossil fuels. There are no real savings associated with electric cars!

Most people who drive electric cars drive them to make themselves feel good and self-righteous. You are not saving the environment by driving an electric car.

Good grief! 90% of the electricity in this country comes from fossil fuels!

Back to the Hammer/Libyan fiasco: The other countries in the Middle East saw what Libya was doing. They began to talk amongst each other. That was the effective beginning of OPEC power.

All Middle East, OPEC member countries begin to tell Exxon and the other companies, 'If you don't give us our price, we're going to shut you down in all the countries.'

(Are you old enough to remember the OPEC Oil Embargo of the 1970's? If you are not, Google it and read- it's worth a look.)

OPEC basically took down the seven sisters, one by one.

Hammer's capitulation started our whole problem. And, if the Seven Sisters had backed him up, he could have told the Libyans to shove it.

It has been terrible for the Western economies and American families, ever since.

The transfer of wealth measured in petro dollars to the Mideast has been unbelievably huge.

There has never been a transfer of such magnitude in the history of mankind. Massive wealth from West to Mid East is being used to our detriment.

Not only do petrodollars ultimately fund terrorism against the West, the loss of jobs and economic activities from production and other ancillary activities that could happen in America, for Americans, could heal and explode our economy, *fast*!

Once again, in the 1970's, we lost another war: The un-declared War…for Oil!"

# Chapter 9

## What Must Be Done to Save America

*(September 16th, 2012, Lesley Stahl of CBS's 60 Minutes Television News Magazine, Interview of Meir Dagan, Former Director of Mossad, Israel's Intelligence Agency)*

*Meir Dagan:*

*I heard very carefully what President Obama said. And he said openly that the military option is on the table, and he is not going to let Iran become a nuclear state.*

*Lesley Stahl:*

*So let me try to sum up what I think you're now saying. And you're saying, "Why should we do it? If we wait and they get the bomb, the Americans will do it."*

*Dagan:*

*The issue of Iran armed with a nuclear capability is not an Israeli problem; it's an international problem.*

*Stahl:*

*So wait and let us do it.*

*Dagan:*

*If I prefer that somebody will do it, I always prefer that Americans will do it.*

-----

"America loves a winner and will not tolerate a loser. This is why America has never, and will never, lose a war."

"May God have mercy upon my enemies because I won't.

*General George S. Patton, Jr.*

----

According to the US Census Bureau, 46,200,000 Americans live in poverty!

45,000,000 are on food stamps. 15,000,000 have been added to the SNAP Program (food stamps) in the last four years.

Fifty percent of Americans pay no income tax.

The top ten percent income earners pay seventy-five percent of total, Federal Income Tax (is that fair? Hell no!).

Forty-seven percent (47%) of Americans are dependent on the government in the form of one or more federal, benefit payments. *(Sources: Standard & Poor's, Office of Management and Budget, U.S.*

*Bureau of Labor Statistics, Morgan Stanley, Joint Committee on Taxation and the U.S. Census.)*

Also, it was known well known, even before Obama Care, that costs of Medicaid are unsustainable!

The numbers of bastard children born in America is ridiculously high and increasing every year.

We are dependent on our enemies for energy.

-----

We must act *immediately* to save this country. We're running out of time! National debt and immorality are compounding at a blinding rate!

**Action Plan**

**1(a):**

In order to get her International Prestige back and to help secure the world against obvious risks, America must take down/destroy any and all nuclear capabilities of Iran!

**1(b):**

For security and to help guarantee success against nuclear, take down operations, America must, simultaneously, take out Iran's offensive, military capabilities; embargo the hell out of them;

and, shut down their export, oil operations until regime change is completed!

America's government officials must realize that this time, there is no option except complete, military victory.

Iran must NOT have nuclear bombs!

While gasoline prices might spike in the short run, there is no need for Americans to worry about supply during the "Neutralize Iran Operation."

The United States of America is in a strong, overall energy position.

Accordingly, see the following Wall Street Journal Article excerpt about global oil and America's strength. The full article can be read at the link just below, http://online.wsj.com/article/SB10000872396390444301704577631820865343432.html?mod=WSJ_WSJ_US_News_6:

*In a conversation with The Wall Street Journal, Daniel Yergin, the energy industry's most prominent chronicler, talks about the American oil renaissance and its profound implications for the U.S. in a changing world. Mr. Yergin, currently vice chairman of IHS, a consulting firm in Englewood, Colo., is the author of "The Quest: Energy, Security, and the Remaking of the Modern*

*World." His history of the oil industry, "The Prize," earned a Pulitzer Prize.*

*Here are edited excerpts from the conversation.*

**Energy Boom**

*WSJ: The U.S. is experiencing an unprecedented boom in oil production. How did this happen? Where is it taking us?*

*MR. YERGIN: The last time we had a presidential election, the U.S. was going to run out of oil. Since then, U.S. oil production has grown about 25%. As has happened in the past, technology has opened doors people didn't know were there or didn't think could be opened.*

*We expect to see tight-oil production [oil extracted from dense rock formations] grow dramatically over the rest of this decade. If you take what's happening in the U.S. and what's happening in Brazil and Canada, we're going to see a rebalancing of global oil flows. By the end of this decade, the Western Hemisphere may be importing very little oil from the Eastern Hemisphere.*

*WSJ: What difference does that make to U.S. oil consumers?*

*MR. YERGIN: Until a couple of years ago, people didn't focus on the economic impact of domestic energy production. Over one million jobs have been created by the development of unconventional gas. It makes the U.S. more competitive. You can see how the growing recognition of the economic impact is changing the political discourse about energy in the U.S., including, very clearly, in the presidential campaign. You would not have had this kind of discussion about energy in 2008.*

*[The new flow] changes the geopolitical perspective about energy. The U.S. is going to be relatively more self-sufficient and less dependent on foreign energy. We're already independent in terms of coal and natural gas; greater reliance on regional and domestic supplies increases our sense of security.*

*WSJ: Will this weaken the U.S.-Saudi relationship?*

*MR. YERGIN: We don't get a lot of our oil from the Middle East as it is today, but the strategic interests are very strong; obviously they're highlighted by continuing tension over Iran's nuclear program...*

*...WSJ: Critics have said the potential of unconventional fields—shale and tight oil—is exaggerated. Is this boom real?*

MR. YERGIN: *The proof is in the numbers. Shale gas (2% of U.S. gas production at the start of the century) is now almost 40% of U.S. gas production. And using this technology in new areas and established oil fields has really revitalized U.S. oil production.*

WSJ: *Can you put this boom in historical perspective?*

MR. YERGIN: *During the oil industry's first century, the U.S. was the world's dominant oil producer. During World War II, six out of seven barrels of oil used by the Allies came from the U.S. After World War II, the U.S. became a net importer of oil, and it was during the 1970s that it came to be a huge importer.*

*The last time we had a presidential campaign, the U.S. seemed set to continue along this path. The only question seemed to be: At what pace would imports grow? Since then, we've seen a big turnaround—from importing 60% of our crude in 2005 to 42% today. This is a big change, and that number will continue to go down as production increases and we continue to be more efficient in terms of the automobiles that we drive.*

*The U.S. is not going to go back to its position as the unquestioned major source of world oil. But our production will continue to grow. It is a great turnaround.*

*WSJ: What sparked it?*

*MR. YERGIN: The main thing here is the new ability to use in oil fields technologies that were developed for shale gas. It's technology and entrepreneurship, initiative, people having different ideas and acting on them...*

Regarding the military operation against Iran, the US must make it clear we have not and will not ask for help. We do not need it.

Our government leaders must make it clear that if any, other countries don't like our plan, they can kiss our ass. USA must make it clear we must deal with this, we will, and after we're done, we'll get back with everyone and we'll all live happily, ever after.

Again, USA should make it clear that the main reasons for the plan are for the USA to regain her prestige because a strong America is good for the world; and, to neutralize the risks to the world, in various ways, associated with the current, Iranian regime.

Parenthetically, as of this writing, there are approximately 20 United States Embassies under protest, even assault. The USA must show the world our country, and/or people, will not be assaulted in any way.

Our leaders must announce, now, that it is now our Policy that if any of our Embassies, Forts, Magazines, or Territories are breached, it will mean automatic WAR!

This should be called our new, Teddy Roosevelt, Big Stick II Policy!

Again, the President of the United States must put out an open letter that essentially says, "If our property or people are assaulted anywhere in the world, the United States Military will put a boot up your ass early in the morning! We have had enough of anti-American protests and attacks!

No other country would put up with treatment of its people like America now allows, e.g. neither Russia, nor China!

**Second:** We must become energy independent! Here's how: We must utilize our own natural resources.

We have the largest, proven coal reserves of any country on the planet (reported as 27% of the world's proven reserves).

We have a 250 year supply of coal, yet we are shutting coal mines down in West Virginia, Virginia, and Pennsylvania (1,200 jobs) because of overly stringent, EPA regulations. Come on,

America! Shutting these mines down is down-right un-American!

You government people modify the regulations so we can get the coal and burn it! China is bringing one coal burning plant on line, everyday!

We have a 100 year supply of natural gas.

We have huge amounts of oil reserves.

Someone explain to me why we're importing (any energy resources)!

Congress must pass and the president must sign, a $20 per barrel tax on foreign oil imports (paid by the oil companies) that specifically goes to pay down the national debt. That's one earmark that would be good for us all!

According to http://www.eia.gov/tools/faqs/faq.cfm?id=727&t=6, the US imports approximately 11.4 million barrels of oil per day. At $20 per barrel (tax), the income applied to pay down the national debt would be $228,000,000 per day.

In addition to rapid debt reduction, our 'Foreign Barrel Tax' tax would incentivize the government to issue domestic drilling permits in the numbers that would match our needs. Permits equal jobs!

Further, the tax would incentivize oil companies to explore and develop *domestic* resources.

It would give alternative energy sources a price advantage for a period long enough period of time for the good and valid ones to get a hold, as appropriate.

We must begin pressing members of Congress and The President, now, because achieving independence will take some time.

This is a tax (and an earmark) upon which everyone can agree! It's good for the Democrats, Republicans, Independents, the 'Green' tree huggers, everyone!

**Third:** We must secure our borders! Not to stop legal immigration; rather, to make sure we have an inventory of smart people because educators in this country have ruined our ability to produce smart people.

We have need for people to fill approximately 20 million high-tech jobs. We don't have the skilled, smart people to fill them!

We are educating waiters, car wash runners, lawn mower operators, and farm laborers!

**Fourth:** We must not let government adopt any policy, or policies, that expand Medicaid and Welfare rolls! Medicaid was already unsustainable, even before the recent run up in the numbers of beneficiaries! Health care costs for the poor via Medicaid alone are enough to financially ruin us!

According to Heritage Foundation calculations based on current and previous Office of Management and Budget documents and other official government sources, when The War on Poverty commenced in 1964, Total Welfare Spending (in Billions of 2008 Dollars) was approximately fifty billion ($50,000,000,000). By 1981, three hundred billion ($300,000,000,000); by 1996, five hundred billion ($500,000,000,000); in 2008, seven hundred billion ($700,000,000,000), and climbing, almost directly vertically!

And food stamps, during Bill Clinton's administration, there were approximately 23 million Americans receiving food stamps; George Bush's, 23.5. But, since Obama entered office, the number has jumped to approximately 39.5 million recipients! Why?

**Fifth:** We must promote high school graduation, marriage, and having children *after* marriage. We must penalize boys and girls, men and women, who have bastard children: No more money for babies! It is clear that government welfare and Medicaid payments incentivize large numbers of women and girls to have additional babies outside of marriage (who are then supported by the labor of working, productive men and women of America)!

**Sixth:** We must make 20% of GDP as the Federal government's maximum debt, by law. Using 20% of GDP as debt limit, the Congress must pass a Balanced Budget Amendment.

Further, to assure legal compliance, the president must have line item veto power. And, he must be legally mandated to use the line item veto to keep on and off budget debt within the 20% of GDP, legal limit!

**Seventh:** It used to be that only property owners could vote. In our present situation, we need to make it law that only people who pay taxes get to vote. Obviously, this would nullify the votes of many people who receive Welfare benefits, food stamps, Medicaid benefits, and other forms of Federal and State governments' assistance. This is as it should be, however, because the status quo incentivizes them to vote for whoever promises to continue to use the productive peoples' money to support them in their poverty. And, it essentially enables them to not try to improve their and their family's lot in the fabric of our society.

**Eighth:** As there is a strong correlation between a lack of education and poverty, schools and teachers must do a better job, or be forced to find other means of making a living. Come on! America's low, world-wide ranking in education is unacceptable! This is America, people! What is wrong with you educators? Your outcomes are truly ridiculous and unacceptable! You wouldn't last two months in private business.

You educators must get on the ball: Top down to every district, educators must agree and begin to execute the strategy and tactic of continually stating to students that the purpose of *their education is for their opportunities! Education is for them!*

# Chapter 10

## What if...

If you are a woman reading this book, what if you pulled up to the gas pump tomorrow and filled up for $2 per gallon.

And, what if you didn't have to work if you didn't want to because inflation was lower so your husband's income was enough (assuming he was not a lay-about and actually worked to provide for his family)?

And, what if, when you went to pick up your children from school, you felt in on their education, you knew they were getting the best education available in the world, and that they would go to college because it was affordable for all?

And, what if your family could afford to take your children to see one of the great, American sites during the summer, every year, so they would grow up with an appreciation of our great land?

And, what if you never, ever, had to feel like you had to apologize to anyone, anywhere in the world, for being an American?

And, what if you knew your home and family were secure?

And, what if you always knew your country was secure?

And, what if you got down right old-fashioned and went back to church, sat with your kids and husband, then went home for lunch and sat at a table, "broke bread" together, and actually talked!

-----

In 1984, the President's Private Sector Survey on Cost Control, also known as The Grace Commission Report, reported to Congress that "…100 percent of what is collected (through the Federal Income Tax) is absorbed solely by interest on the federal debt and by federal government contributions to transfer payments. In other words, all individual income tax revenues are gone before one nickel is spent on the services [that] taxpayers expect from their government."
http://www.uhuh.com/taxstuff/gracecom.htm

Congress did nothing about the recommendations of the commission to curb debt and interest. That was approximately 28 years ago!

All our 'money' is borrowed into existence.

None of the "What if's" above can, or ever will, happen again in America if we don't execute our recommendations in the last chapter.

We will be consumed by the costs of our indigenous poor, and interest to the private, Federal Reserve Bank and bond holders!

Tell others about this little, pink book!

**Join the national conversation!**

**@HotPinkBook**

**www.facebook.com/HotPinkBook**

Made in the USA
Charleston, SC
12 December 2012

change. The degree and speed of his change was startling. Of course, he had it all thought out.

As I said, he was almost perfect until we married. The day we married, all his rules changed. I thought he was joking but he wasn't.

Now that I'm not married, I do not date right now. Why do I not date? Well, for men these days, it's all about the form of control, and games. And, they cannot communicate.

They don't communicate well; yet, they always want to go to bed with you as their primary goal. They always have a goal.

Once they have that, it's all different. From there, it's all about control.

It's all about control. I can't stress that enough!

I have thought long and hard about this: Their desire to control comes from the fact <u>that men lost control years ago</u>. So what they can exert on a personal level is all the control they can have, now (Underline added because interviewee emphatically spoke the point).

Here's a pretty good example of what's going on out there right now in our age group. A friend of mine decided to use online dating. While online dating can work, my friend's experiences